Hidden in the Cleft

A Journey of Discovering My True Identity in Christ

Dorothy Caldwell

Hidden in the Cleft © 2020 by Dorothy Caldwell. All Rights Reserved.

All rights reserved. No part of this book may be reproduced in any form or by any electronic or mechanical means including information storage and retrieval systems, without permission in writing from the author. The only exception is by a reviewer, who may quote short excerpts in a review.

Scripture quotations marked AMPC are taken from the Amplified® Bible, Copyright © 1954, 1958, 1962, 1964, 1965, 1987 by The Lockman Foundation. Used by permission. www.Lockman.org

Scripture quotations marked MSG are taken from *THE MESSAGE*, copyright © 1993, 2002, 2018 by Eugene H. Peterson. Used by permission of NavPress. All rights reserved. Represented by Tyndale House Publishers, Inc.

Scripture quotations marked NKJV taken from the New King James Version®. Copyright © 1982 by Thomas Nelson. Used by permission. All rights reserved.

Scripture quotations marked NLT are taken from the *Holy Bible*, New Living Translation, copyright © 1996, 2004, 2015 by Tyndale House Foundation. Used by permission of Tyndale House Publishers, Inc., Carol Stream, Illinois 60188. All rights reserved.

Cover designed by Justin M. Carey Designs

Printed in the United States of America

First Printing: February 2021
The Scribe Tribe Publishing Group

ISBN-978-1-7352568-8-7 (print)
IBSN-978-1-7352568-9-4 (electronic)

This book is dedicated to the woman who not only gave me life, but gave me LIFE, through Jesus Christ – Dorothy Custard. Momma, I am only who I am today because of your relentless love for me and the God that you knew and loved. I can only hope and pray that this is a small testimony of just how precious and special a wife, mother, grandmother, sister, aunt, and awesome in-love-with-Jesus woman that you were to me, and all who knew you. My heart, my soul, my spirit misses you every day. I love you forever.

    – My life: a love song for you and unto our Lord! Amen.

Contents

Foreword 2
Introduction 4
Rise Up, ... 6
Phenomenal Woman 6
Unforgiven 8
The Day Doesn't Matter 11
Psalm 34 13
Life of Fasting 16
I Am Loved! 17
Ecclesiastes 3:11 21
A Beautiful Tapestry 23
I Am a Battle Axe 26
Police Woman 29
Leading by Following 32
Say Yes! 34
Embracing Who I Am 38
Give Me a Clean Heart 41
Consistency of Character 43
Impact 46
On Mondays 49
Let It Go! 51
My Love Song to Him 54
A Mighty Whirlwind 57
What Do You See? 59
What Do You See? 61
My Autopilot Kicked In 64
Choose to Rest & 67
Rejoice In Jesus 67
Full Circle 69
Yet Will I Praise Him 73

Be Persistent in Faith	76
Hidden in the Cleft	80
of the Rock	80
Dry Clean Only	83
Burning Both Candles at the End with a Stick	85
It's Just My Angel	88
Breaking Forth	91
Wind Beneath My Wings	94
Country Girl	97
His Covenant is Eternal	99
He Danced with Me	102
Ascending with Him	105
Seated with Him	107
Obedience is Key	109
Expectation &	112
Hunger Fulfilled	112
It Gets Smaller	114
He Goes Before You	117
Be On Guard	120
Let His Glory Arise!	123
I Feel Like Running	126
Epilogue	129
Acknowledgements	131
Meet the Author	132

Foreword

I always had a belief in the power of relationships. As a child, I spent a lot of time with my paternal grandparents. Their marriage, family structure, parenting teamwork, and community status were appealing to me. My time with them propelled my desire to become a relationship coach. I have been counseling and coaching couples since I completed grad school almost 25 years ago. My husband is a former NFL player and team chaplain for the Chicago Bears. We have worked with all types of couples from athletes to executives. During our five-year stint working with the Bears, I had the pleasure of meeting my dear friend, Dorothy Caldwell.

It's been 10 years since I met Dorothy. Our mutual love for Jesus and dance is what made our satellites intercept. What an interesting season of life it was for me. Spiritually, I was carrying a lot of hurt with great uncertainty of where it would lead me. Then came Dorothy. Like a strong wind of refreshment and promise, the Lord brought me someone special to help me heal in a unique way specified for me. Her combination of love for others and unmeasurable faith in God made our relationship heaven sent. Our spirits aligned personally, spiritually, and professionally. We became so connected we began to affectionately refer to each other as David and Jonathan.

When I think of Dorothy Caldwell four words come to mind: resilient, disciplined, faithful, and courageous. As you read *Hidden in the Cleft*, you will gain insight into the various valley lows and mountain highs Dorothy has experienced in her life. Through it all she has remained the same. She is a lover of God like none other. She loves God's people firmly and consistently with great compassion and biblical truth. She is determined to exhibit excellence in all her endeavors. She walks boldly into every season of life because of her faith and trust in God. Dorothy is a leader to her core. She's the kind of leader with whom I am sure the Father is well pleased.

As you read *Hidden in the Cleft*, you will find yourself on a colorful journey through Dorothy's life experiences. My hope is that you will open yourself up to hear her heart, feel her joy, encounter her sorrow, embrace her faith, acquire her courage, and allow her love for God to pierce your heart. This book challenged me, encouraged me, affirmed me, and moved me to re-evaluate my relationship with God once again and level up my pursuit of Him ensuring that I am the most confident and secure in my faith than I have previously been. Dorothy is a constant reminder that we can always love Him more, serve Him more, and believe in Him more.

Thank you Dorothy for such a beautiful encounter with both you and God.

With a heart full of love for my forever David--

Your forever Jonathan,
Michelle McElroy

Introduction

Moses was called, appointed, and anointed by God to lead the Children of Israel out of Egypt into the *Promised Land*, but did you know Moses was not a willing servant initially? Moses, after discovering his identity, began to show signs of his insecurity issues early on in his spiritual journey when he overreacted, killed a man, and fled to Midian. Thinking he could escape his past and his call, Moses pushed his people and their freedom out of his thoughts and purposed to live his best life in Midian. God knew that He was going to have to do something dramatic to get Moses attention, *again*. And I would say, a burning bush was dramatic enough, wouldn't you agree?

Although Moses had literally been saved by divine intervention, was raised in the house of Pharaoh, was hand-picked by God, and dwelled in Midian for 40 years, he still was not confident in himself and/or his abilities to do and finish the task that God revealed and asked him to do. No, Moses was not a confident man. He was insecure and could not see *why* God chose him, and he couldn't see *what* God saw in him. But God! He knew, and He did not allow the inhibitions, pushbacks, and concerns of Moses to keep him from his God-ordained purpose. *(Shouting right now!)* God – who is loving, kind and patient – gave Moses a Fatherly push toward his destiny, walking him through a beautiful journey and discovery of 1) knowing who He was in God's eyes 2) knowing the sovereignty and Fatherhood of God and 3) knowing this GOD, his Abba Father, in an intimate way. It was an intimacy that no one else had experienced (before Jesus). He was the only person throughout the Bible, and history, that could see and experience the awe and splendor of God's Glory. Pause and think about that. Wow!

So, why this story? Why Moses? Because I believe that my life has paralleled Moses' in so many ways and I believe that this book will reflect that journey. Yes! I totally relate to Moses on many levels. I connect with all that he was, his struggles of survival to just live, his fears, his bad decisions, his inhibitions and his insecurities, and his pushback to God. I, too, couldn't understand *why* God chose me and *what* He saw in me! But just like I relate to the insecurities, I also relate to the journey and beauty of being gently nudged and challenged by God to go, grow, and do. I have also experienced the wars, the standing in faith, and the victories of a great God in my life. I have come to know and understand how God sees me, understand His sovereignty and Him as my Father, and to know Him more intimately than I ever thought fathomable.

When I began this journey of writing I had no idea I would be putting this in a book or print form. I thought I was doing a blog just to be doing something (lol). My reasons for writing were more therapeutic than purpose. Little did I know God had ordained the reverse. When I received the *Hidden In the Cleft of the Rock* download, it was at one of the most challenging times in my life. The things I was writing were more out of faith than out what I was experiencing in my life at the time. I had no idea that one blog entry would get the most hits of all my writings over the ten years it's been in existence. Even today, I still receive emails and notes from those who come upon it, writing to speak of how it blessed them. I take no credit; all glory to the Lord from whom it flowed.

However, I must say that's the reason that I am writing this preface today. It is the reason I am functional in full-time ministry. It is the reason that I am praying, laying hands, prophesying, preaching, and teaching. It is the reason that I continue to press past insecurities and inhibitions every day. (Yes, they still rear their heads.) A loving Father, who out of His love and patience for me, chose to place me in the *Cleft of the Rock* (Jesus Christ), so that I can get a glimpse of His Glory, is the reason I am. 'No' was never an option, and I am thankful that He did not, and has not, given up on me. That's a love that I struggle to fully comprehend, but that I am ever learning to embrace.

As you read these pages, my prayer for you is that you will be able to tangibly feel and experience the depth and love that the Father has for you. I pray that whatever you're facing right now or may be going through that you won't give up. I pray that whatever God is challenging you to do that seems impossible to be done, you will yield to the process. **His yoke is easy, and His burdens are light.** And finally, I pray that if you don't know that you find the eternal life that is *Hidden in the Cleft of the Rock*, Jesus Christ.

This is my love song to Him!

Rise Up, Phenomenal Woman

"Wherefore I also, after I heard of your faith in the Lord Jesus, and love unto all the saints, I cease not to give thanks for you, making mention of you in my prayers." ~Ephesians 1:15-16 KJV

It was at least 25 years ago when the Lord burned into my heart a passion for women's ministry. At the time I was very young, newly married, and a new mother. Although I had grown up in the church and been around ministry for years, I had no idea of how to "do" ministry. I remember wrestling with the Lord over the idea, saying to Him, "What can a young girl, barely wet behind the ears, have to say to women? Better yet, who would even listen?!" Well, the Lord won that battle and Hannah Women's Ministries was born in my home in 1993. There were three young women in attendance: Dawn M., Teresa M., and Vanessa B. Those brave women, who are still dear friends of mine to this day, came to hear this young woman share her heart and relationship with Jesus. I don't know if I imparted anything useful that day, as I can barely remember the details. But what I do remember is that the presence of the Lord showed up and confirmed a birthing in me that is still going to this day. Hannah Ministries has long been done away with, but the deep passion and heart for women continues to burn in my heart and is even increasing daily.

You see, this passion I have for the women of God is one that I can't shake, no matter how hard I try. I have a passion to see them set free from the lies and deceit of the enemy that is so prevalent in many today. I have a passion to see them rise and be a voice of the Lord in the earth through word and deed. I have a passion to see Jesus exalted in the life of every woman I meet. This passion compels me to stretch beyond my comfort zone. (This book is outside that comfort zone!) It compels me to be open and transparent, sharing the secrets of my heart in hopes of helping other women come to know His great love.

This passion compels me to intercede daily on behalf of the beautiful women He has placed in my circle. It compels me to pray that they are strengthened in Him, filled with His spirit, and graced with the ability to stand in whatever situation they are in. It compels me to pray diligently and fervently that every woman come to know who they are in Christ Jesus and that they walk boldly in the authority that they are given. It compels me to go to war, in prayer, confrontation, and right teaching, against the plans of the enemy to slander the reputation and hearts of women by causing them to make "silly women" decisions. It compels me to pray that every woman would rise and be Godly wives, mothers, and sisters in the earth, walking in the wisdom of the Lord.

To the women reading this, know that I'm praying even now that your hearts are stirred as you turn the pages of this book. Know that whatever situation you're in, it is not the final word on your future. Remember that the Father, who is full of grace and mercy, has a plan for your life. I speak to you today, "Rise up, woman of God! Take your rightful place in the Kingdom. Rise up and be the phenomenal woman that He has called you to be, forgetting the past and pressing forward in Him. Know that I love you and that my heart beats to see His glory fulfilled in your life. Amen."

Unforgiven

"In whom we have redemption through his blood, the forgiveness of sins, according to the riches of his grace..."
~Ephesians 1:7 NIV

I love non-fictional action-drama movies. You know the ones where the main character is slightly imperfect, but by some means of adrenaline and pure drive, can get themselves out of deadly situations. I love these characters because they are usually strong, smart, witty, resourceful, and sometimes cute (lol). Although I've seen a few love stories and enjoyed them, they are not my first pick at the box office. Give me movies like the *Bourne Identity, Bourne Supremacy, Bourne Ultimatum*, any of the *Die Hard* Series, *Lethal Weapon I, II, III, & IV, Ironman,* and *The Book of Eli* any day. One of my all-time favorite movies is *Unforgiven*, with Clint Eastwood and Morgan Freeman. I absolutely love that movie!

The movie was about a man named William Munny, played by Eastwood, who was a widower with two young children. He used to be a very vicious gunfighter, but after marrying gave up gunfighting, drinking, and most other vices. His wife, the catalyst of change in his life, died of smallpox in 1878, but he continued to try to eke out a living with his children on their hog farm, and to tried to be the kind of man he believed his late wife would have wanted him to be. In the movie, Munny takes on one last job: retrieving an outlaw for pay. Munny recruits his former gun-slinging partner, Ned, played by Freeman, to help with the quest. They partner with a young, ignorant, half-blind gunslinger who, along with the town Sheriff-Villain, ends up making what should have been a simple quest, complicated. Without giving the whole movie away, numerous events happened that led to the revelation of Munny's former life. Word spread quickly of his former evils and the showdown was set to take place. You will have to watch the movie to find out what happened. It's worth the time, I promise.

This movie came rushing back to me when I was dealing with a personal situation. It seemed that my past was again resurfacing, unsolicited. For a quick minute, I felt like the Munny character from the movie. I just can't get a break from the past, no matter what I do. No matter how much I live right, my past seems to always be looming there, waiting to pounce on me. I will be the first to confess, that I have not lived a perfect, sinless life. I have made mistakes that have brought pain and hurt to me and others. As a matter of fact, I seem to mess up some kind of way every day, needing His grace to love and sustain me once again. But as I said, I felt that condemnation, but only for a quick minute because the Holy Spirit was on the job, as usual. The scripture promises us that the Holy Spirit would lead us into all truth (John 16:13) and bring all things (truths) to our remembrance (John 14:26). Just as quickly as the condemnation of my past came, the reminder of my forgiveness and redemption through the blood of Jesus resounded from the Holy Spirit. Hallelujah!

The Holy Spirit began to flood my spirit with reminders of Jesus' love for me. He reminded me that my past is just that, the past. And although man holds on and tries to get you to do the same, our heavenly Father remembers it no more. The scripture promises that He would remove our iniquities far from us: ***"As far as the east is from the west, so far hath he removed our transgressions from us." (Psalm 103:12)*** Our sins of the past are thrown into the sea of forgetfulness when Jesus is Lord of our life.

I am rejoicing as I am reminded today that I am a sinner, forgiven by a gracious Father. (Ephesians 2:8) I am a sinner, redeemed by the precious shed blood of the Lord Jesus Christ. (Colossians 1:14) I am a sinner, no longer under condemnation, but under grace. (Romans 8:1) I am a sinner, walking in His loving kindness and His tender mercies. (Lamentations 3:22-23) I'm reminded that I am no longer bound by sin, no longer attached to my past, but free to live for Him. (Romans 6) All praise, honor and glory be to Him!

For those of you who know Jesus as personal Lord and Savior, be free today. Let your past be the past. Know that you are forgiven. Old things have passed away and all is new. (2 Corinthians 5:17) You are a new creature (a totally transformed being) in Him. Your yesterday is not your today and does not determine your tomorrow.

If you don't know the love of Jesus personally and He is not Lord of your life, I admonish you to ask Him into your heart today. Know that you too can be set free from your past. You no longer have to live under the condemnation of mistakes and hurts of the past. The Lord Jesus loves and desires to have a personal relationship with you. He wants to give you a new life in him, one that is abundant. (John 10:10) Receive His gift today!

"That if thou shalt confess with thy mouth the Lord Jesus, and shalt believe in thine heart that God hath raised him from the dead, thou shalt be saved. For with the heart man believeth unto righteousness; and with the mouth confession is made unto salvation." ~Romans 10:9-10 KJV

The Day Doesn't Matter

"Now upon the first day of the week, very early in the morning, they came unto the sepulchre, bringing the spices which they had prepared, and certain others with them. And they found the stone rolled away from the sepulchre. And they entered in, and found not the body of the Lord Jesus." Luke 24:1-3 KJV

Each year as Holy Week approaches and we begin the celebration of Jesus' sacrifice at the cross of Calvary, there is no shortage of debates. I have chosen not to get into religious arguments over the fact that many "Christian" holidays are rooted in paganism (and they are). I know that Easter Sunday, which I choose to call Resurrection Sunday, is based on the worship of the sun. That's why it changes every year. I had to contend with those facts over the years as I've had to answer many questions from my extremely inquisitive children. I always gave them Truth as an answer, making them aware of the fact that there is no Easter bunny nor is there a Santa Claus coming down the chimney at Christmas.

However, I have also chosen not to swing to the other side of the pendulum and throw everything out with the bathwater either. Although, I did try that for a year, and it didn't work out too well. I have since learned to rest in Him and just do as the word of God says -- to love the Lord with all my heart, soul, mind, and strength every day! I have put my religious, Pharisee and Sadducee attitude on the shelf and decided to celebrate Jesus today, tomorrow, next week, Good Friday, Resurrection Sunday, Christmas, and for always.

I choose to celebrate Jesus because the truth is that no matter which day we designate as His birth, His death at Calvary, or His day of resurrection, the fact is that HE WAS born of a virgin (Mary); HE DID live on this earth 33 years; HE WAS baptized by John the Baptist, the Holy Spirit DID ASCEND upon Him like a dove; HE DID do miracles and wonders in the earth; HE WAS betrayed; HE WAS falsely arrested and falsely accused; HE WAS beaten all night; HE WAS spit on; HE DID wear a crown of thorns upon His head; HE WAS forced to carry His cross to Calvary; HE WAS pierced in His side; HE WAS given vinegar to drink on the cross; HE DID hang on the cross for three hours; HE DID die and was buried in Joseph's tomb; HE DID lay in that tomb for three days; HIS tomb stone WAS rolled away by the angel of the Lord; HE DID ARISE FROM THE DEAD; HE DID appear to His disciples; HE DID ascend into heaven as they watched, and HE NOW SITS at the right hand of the Father making intercession for US! Hallelujah!

    Frankly, I don't care which day is the actual day that Jesus was born, died or arose. I only care that there was a day and that He is alive *this* day. Since the above facts are true, I will celebrate Him today, tomorrow, Sunday, and for all eternity. Amen and amen. I pray that you will celebrate Him as well, not just on Resurrection Sunday or Christmas, but every day. And if you have not given your heart to Him, do so, and do it quickly. Oh, how He loves you and me!

Psalm 34

"I will bless the Lord at all times: his praise shall continually be in my mouth." ~Psalm 34:1 KJV

I love King David and the book of Psalms. Whether I am rejoicing, crying, hurting, disappointed, dismayed, discouraged, inspired, or excited, I can always find a Psalm that speaks to my heart. Maybe because David was a warrior and a worshipper, two things that I can really relate to. Whatever the reason, I love the writer and the book.

I love the fact that I can find scriptures from thousands of years ago that relate to me and any situation that I may be facing in 2020. Imagine that! It baffles the mind to think of how things have advanced since the time of Jesus. Can you imagine life before television, cell phones, and laptops? Yet, His Word has stood the test of time and is still able to transform lives. The Word of God is living and is powerful to save to the utmost. (Hebrews 4:12) Hallelujah!

One morning, as I began to write, one of my favorite Psalms rose in my spirit. Before I knew it, I was speaking, and eventually writing out, the whole Psalm. In this Psalm, David was expressing the faithfulness of the Lord and showing the comparison between the plight of the wicked and of those that belong to God. The words spoke to my heart and reminded me just how much my Father loves us, His people. He loves us more than our finite minds can comprehend. He is always thinking of us and will move the heavens on our behalf. Even when it seems that He is distant and has seemingly forgotten us, He is yet being faithful to us.

When I am counseling, I often tell people, "Just because you don't see God moving doesn't mean that He isn't moving. He is always working things for your good." After all, the Word of God tells us that we know in part and we prophesy in part. (I Corinthians 13:9) Only the Father God knows the whole story. Only He knows the beginning from the end. And although He gives us glimpses of our future at times, only He really knows the results.

The Father also knows that we are weak and that we are oftentimes afraid, discouraged and even impatient with Him. That's why He has given us His Word and the Holy Spirit to help us. It is in the Word of God that we can find answers for those times of fear, discouragement, and impatience. The Holy Spirit, our Paraclete, is waiting to guide and direct us to the Word of God for edification, exhortation, comfort, and sometimes correction. All we need to do is ask. I dare you to read His Word and seek Him today. Then watch and see the transforming power of the Word of God.

I have so many scriptures that I meditate on regularly in both the Old and New Testament. These scriptures have walked me through many seasons of my life. I am so thankful for the Word of God. My prayer today is that you will take time to read your Bible today. Ask the Holy Spirit to give you a scripture specifically for you and your situation. You will be amazed at the accuracy of the Spirit of God. God really does know your heart. When you cry out to Him, He will answer. Until then, I pray that this Psalm blesses you the same way that it blesses me.

Psalm 34
I will bless the LORD at all times: his praise shall continually be in my mouth.
My soul shall make her boast in the LORD: the humble shall hear thereof, and be glad.
O magnify the LORD with me, and let us exalt his name together.
I sought the LORD, and he heard me, and delivered me from all my fears.
They looked unto him, and were lightened: and their faces were not ashamed.
This poor man cried, and the LORD heard him, and saved him out of all his troubles.
The angel of the LORD encampeth round about them that fear him, and delivereth them.
O taste and see that the LORD is good: blessed is the man that trusteth in him.
O fear the LORD, ye his saints: for there is no want to them that fear him.

The young lions do lack, and suffer hunger: but they that seek the LORD shall not want any good thing.
Come, ye children, hearken unto me: I will teach you the fear of the LORD.
What man is he that desireth life, and loveth many days, that he may see good?
Keep thy tongue from evil, and thy lips from speaking guile.
Depart from evil, and do good; seek peace, and pursue it.
The eyes of the LORD are upon the righteous, and his ears are open unto their cry.
The face of the LORD is against them that do evil, to cut off the remembrance of them from the earth.
The righteous cry, and the LORD heareth, and delivereth them out of all their troubles.
The LORD is nigh unto them that are of a broken heart; and saveth such as be of a contrite spirit.
Many are the afflictions of the righteous: but the LORD delivereth him out of them all.
He keepeth all his bones: not one of them is broken.
Evil shall slay the wicked: and they that hate the righteous shall be desolate.
The LORD redeemeth the soul of his servants: and none of them that trust in him shall be desolate.

Life of Fasting

"Therefore also now, saith the Lord, turn ye even to me with all your heart, and with fasting, and with weeping, and with mourning..." ~Joel 2:12 KJV

When I laid down for bed at midnight, I knew that I had a marathon day ahead. It was a day full of dance classes, rehearsals, errands, and loads of responsibilities to take care of. It's on those types of mornings that I have two cups of coffee to get me going. Normally, I would have pumped myself on caffeine and took on the day, but that wasn't an option that morning.

I was in the last two days of a 21-day church wide fast, so there was no caffeine for me on the menu. I was determined to finish well, so I leaned hard on the Lord that day. I refused to let His faithfulness be secondary to my caffeine. I trusted the Father to empower me by His Spirit and to give me strength and wisdom. I trusted the Holy Spirit, my Paraclete, to be my guide and to lead me into all truth.

Now, I know that this is how I (we) should walk every day, right?! That's why I love fasting. It reveals all our crutches and lean posts--those things that we lean on and rely on to get us through whatever. When you're fasting, you must shift your dependence. Your daily reliance cannot be focused on food, people, and even caffeine. Your trust must be in Him. It's a faith walk, and that's a good thing.

My prayer for you today is that you would continue to live a life of fasting, making it a lifestyle and not just an annual event. You only gain when you live a life of denial. When you deny yourself, you gain so much of Him (Mark 8:36, John 12:25). The Father loves us and desires to extend His grace and mercy to us every day. Hallelujah!

I Am Loved!

Oh, how He loves you and me,
Oh, how He loves you and me!
He gave His life, what more could He give?
Oh, how He loves you,
Oh, how He love me,
Oh, how He loves you and me!

This song was on my heart for several days. I was singing it in my spirit as I was going about the many demands of my life. I am intentional about declaring some things over my life and one of those declarations is simply that *I am loved*. I know that might seem like an unusual confession, especially for a married woman with children who is constantly surrounded by people. If I were on the outside looking in and lacking discernment, I would probably think the same thing. However, through the last several years of pruning and testing from the Lord, I found that my heart began to lose focus of the simple fact that *I am loved*.

The circumstances of life had become so dim and heavy at one point that it took me to a place of despair and borderline depression. My heart was sinking fast, wondering and asking the Lord how long must I endure that dreadful place of desolation. I felt like King David in Psalm 13. My heart was heavy, yet I knew my hope was in the Lord. The constant demands of life, that seemingly were being met at the twelfth hour, were stressful to say the least. At some point, I looked up and found that my weary soul had veered off focus. I began to whine, *"Why me, Lord?"* which of course, was the intention of the enemy all along. He desired to cause me to change my focus. And in a moment of weariness, I did just that.

Weariness is a dangerous state of being if your flesh has not been disciplined. That one little thought caused bells to ring in the enemy's camp. I can imagine the demonic forces being summoned together to be given dispatching orders on the fresh bait. I believe the enemy waits to pounce on such thinking, ready to give plenty of answers, none of which will be the truth. I opened the door for the enemy to bombard my mind with additional supporting thoughts by not bringing that thought of *"Why me?"* under subjection to the Word of God. That one thought led me down a road that quickly became a slippery slope into despair.

For this very reason, I always make a point to teach and preach on **II Corinthians 10:5, *"Casting down imaginations and every high thing that exalteth itself against the knowledge of God, and bringing into captivity every thought to the obedience of Christ."*** The enemy will take your one thought and magnify it, sometimes causing a stronghold or a root of bitterness to be established in your heart and that's a dangerous and difficult state to be in. Our focus must remain on Jesus. The enemy intended, with some success, to get my focus off the heart of Jesus *for* me and *towards* me. For a moment, I lost focus of the fact that the Father's ultimate purpose of this time of pruning and testing in my life was so that I might *bear more fruit*:

"Every branch in me that beareth not fruit he taketh away: and every branch that beareth fruit, he purgeth it, that it may bring forth more fruit." ~John 15:2 KJV

Instead of seeing the great harvest that was to come I began to focus on evaluating and valuing (quantifying) myself. I began to judge my life based on my external circumstances. How foolish! Understand that I was not ignorant of the enemy's devices. He has been deceiving and lying to the saints for thousands of years. You would think that I would have quickly recognized what was taking place and dealt with it. In a perfect *Walgreen's* world that would have happened.

∞ ∞ ∞

Side note --- The enemy, the devil, Lucifer, or whatever name you choose to use, *is* a worthy foe. And neither you nor I should ever think for one minute that we can outwit him without the wisdom of the Holy Spirit. He is smarter than you and me (I say that loosely), yet he is no match for our Father. *"My Daddy can beat your daddy!"* Praise be to the Father for giving us the Holy Spirit. Not just to guide, but to guide us into all truth. We can be confident that no matter what the enemy attempts to do in our lives, the Holy Spirit is always there to help and give us a way of escape.

"There hath no temptation taken you but such as is common to man: but God is faithful, who will not suffer you to be tempted above that ye are able; but will with the temptation also make a way to escape, that ye may be able to bear it." ~I Corinthians 10:13 KJV

The enemy had me. I went down an ugly road of rehashing mistakes, bad decisions, good decisions, missed opportunities, and seemingly non-existent opportunities. I evaluated my marriage, my kids, my family, and my ministry. You name it, I evaluated it. In the end I came up short. *No kidding?!*

Of course, this was right where the enemy wanted me -- looking at myself. I swallowed that foolish thinking and allowed myself to feel devalued and unloved. Then one day while I was in prayer sobbing over my "distresses," I received a Holy Spirit slap in the face. *Those really wake you up!* The Lord, in His kind and gentle way, began to rebuke and correct my stinking thinking. I cried, repented, cried some more, repented some more, and then got up off my face. It took a minute, but in the end, I was refocused on Him. I determined that day that no matter how things looked, or how bad they seemed, I was going to declare truth over myself, my family, and my circumstances.

I adopted a phrase that I have used as a past Facebook signature: "I AM Positioned for Greatness in Him: Focused. Inspired. Excited. Determined. LOVED." I believe these words with all my heart. Every time I write or say them my spirit comes into agreement with the Spirit of the

Lord. I believe that these mere words, although powerless in and of themselves, spoken in faith bring an eternal change in my heart even in the natural. If nothing else, it reminds me of my eternal truth and keeps me focused on the one that truly LOVES me, Jesus Christ.

Oh, how He loves you and me!

Ecclesiastes 3:11

"He hath made every thing beautiful in his time..."
~Ecclesiastes 3:11KJV

I love to look good and dress well! Don't act like you're so shocked by that statement; so do you! I love wearing nice clothes, nice shoes and smelling good. Anytime I leave my home, whether it's to go to a business lunch or to the local grocery store, I do my best to be coordinated, crisp and clean, with three-inch heels in tote. If I had my druthers, I would spend all my extra money on cologne, long coats, and high heels. That's just who I am!

People dress the way they do for different reasons: job requirements, status, image, position, and some, just because they got it like that and can. I'm not mad at any of them. However, for me, my dress is much more than that. There is a purpose behind it. Yes, it's fun, but my real purpose is to be a display of His glory in the earth. I purpose to be an outward expression of love, from an inward transformation of grace. Understand that I'm not condoning any kind of prideful exhibition or selfish ambition. I'm simply saying your outward expression can either reflect the glory of the Lord upon you or a reflection of your hurt and pain.

A merry heart maketh a cheerful countenance: but by sorrow of the heart the spirit is broken. ~Proverbs 15:13 KJV

When I was a very young girl, I was molested continuously for many years. As a result of those violations, I lived with shame and condemnation throughout my adolescent and early adult years. Instead of being strong and confident, I lived as a very timid and scared young child and woman. Every day I hid in the invisible shells created by my insecurities and fears, many times being alone and friendless. I spent my days looking at the floor and hiding behind the person in front of me, hoping not to be seen or heard. I remember my 9th grade year when I could wear makeup thinking to myself, "This is my saving grace. Now I can put on this beautiful *fake* face to hide my ugly real face." Yet every day, still feeling deep inside my heart that I was an ugly duckling that would never fulfill her purpose and become a beautiful swan.

Praise God for deliverance and freedom! The Father graced me to meet some powerful people of God who, through the power of the Holy Spirit, set me free. These men and women of God took me under their wings and ministered to my heart, breaking the spirit of shame and guilt off my life. They ministered to my broken and crushed spirit by embracing me and loving me, even when I was unlovable. They opened their hearts to me, shared their personal victories and gave me hope for a future. These great men and women of God spoke words of life to a broken vessel bringing healing to my heart and soul. I'm grateful for their labor of love towards me. I'm living my purpose today because of them.

Yes, I still love to wear makeup and dress to the nines -- no longer to cover up, but only to enhance the true beauty that was once stolen and is now returned to me.

What is your look displaying? What is your countenance speaking to others? When you look in the mirror and see yourself, what do you see? Do you see a new creature in Christ Jesus? Do you see a child of God redeemed by grace? Or do you see the pain and ugliness of your past? Do you see abuse, neglect, abandonment, betrayal, incest, fornication, alcoholism, or drug abuse? Perhaps you see a person trapped by your circumstance. The word of God says, **"Therefore if any man be in Christ, he is a new creature: old things are passed away; behold, all things are become new." (2 Corinthians 5:17)**

Be encouraged, my brothers and sisters! Jesus is still in the business of healing and setting the captive free. If He did it for me; surely, He can do it for you! Know that there's nothing that is too horrible or too deep that He cannot heal and His love cannot cover. All you need do is ask. Call on Him today and see won't He answer. Be free, today. In Jesus' name!

A Beautiful Tapestry

"I will praise thee; for I am fearfully and wonderfully made: marvellous are thy works; and that my soul knoweth right well."
~Psalm 139:14 KJV

I can't! I can't change it! No matter how hard I desire it, think on it, dwell on it, look at pictures, talk to friends, and even pray over it, I can't change it! My past is written in eternity and there's nothing I can do to make it different.

My life has been no bed of roses but when I look back, I can clearly see the grace of the Father swirling through all the ups and downs that have come my way. The one thing, or should I say, the one person that has been a constant voice of peace, grace, and mercy has been my mother, Dorothy Custard. This is a woman who brings me to tears just thinking of her. Not just because she's my mother and not because she's been perfect, but because she gave me the gift of life--my natural life, as well as my spiritual one. My mother introduced me to Jesus at a very young age and because of her teaching and display of the love of Jesus, I wanted to receive Him as my personal savior and be baptized in His name. At the age of six, I did just that.

I didn't get baptized at a pretty, little church with all the nice bells and whistles that I see today. I was baptized at an old theater that had been turned into a church. The pastor at that time was the late Reverend Nathan Woods. The church smelled of mildew all the time, probably because the roof was always leaking. And no matter how bright it was outside, it was always very dark inside. It could be that it was meant for watching movies! The baptismal pool did not have a set place; most of the time it sat in the front of the sanctuary on the right side, ready for baptism at any time. It was painted dark blue or black and it was very old and unkempt.

I remember standing at the top of the ladder at the edge of the entrance into the baptismal pool. It was like looking down into a black hole. The reverend could see that I was a little nervous or scared, so he said to me, "Don't be afraid." As he tugged my hand gently, I began to make my descent down the inner steps into the dark, dark waters. It was like I was literally living the word: being put to death so that I could live eternally with Him. (Romans 6:3)

The pastor covered my face with a cloth and pulled me back into the waters. When he brought me back up, all I could do was cry. I didn't really know why I was crying; it was probably the presence of the Lord upon me because He was indeed there. All I know for sure is that I was no longer in the kingdom of darkness; I was officially a part of the kingdom of God.

This is a beautiful memory for me that I cherish. The impact it has had on my life is almost indescribable. I believe the greater impact is yet to be seen. I am sharing this because as I said at the beginning, my past is written in eternity and there's nothing I can do to make it different. Every day I arise to give thanks to my Father, who once again extended new mercies for the day. (Lamentations 3:22-23) At the same time, our adversary, the accuser of the brethren, our enemy, the devil, tries his best to get me to dwell on the mistakes and failures of yesterday. Sometimes he makes them so big and magnified that they almost out shadow God's grace and mercy. Don't fall for the trick! Yes, we all have made mistakes, whether ten years ago or ten minutes ago, but all is covered under the blood of Jesus. Look again and see God's hand of mercy and grace. See the times of His faithfulness interwoven throughout your life. Enjoy those moments and know that all else is covered in Him.

Remember, when the Father sees you, He sees His son, Jesus Christ. (Philippians 3:9) We are His workmanship in Christ Jesus (Ephesians 2:10), and He is forming us into the image of His dear son, Jesus Christ, every day. The imperfections of our past are just that, the past. All has been forgiven for those who are in Christ Jesus. The Father, who is the master weaver, has taken the mistakes and failures of our past and interwoven them with His grace, mercy and love and created a beautiful tapestry for all the world to see: you!

Finally, brethren, whatsoever things are true, whatsoever things are honest, whatsoever things are just, whatsoever things are pure, whatsoever things are lovely, whatsoever things are of good report; if there be any virtue, and if there be any praise, think on these things.
~Philippians 4:8 KJV

I Am a Battle Axe

"Thou art my battle axe and weapons of war: for with thee will I break in pieces the nations, and with thee will I destroy kingdoms." ~Jeremiah 51:20 KJV

In December of 2009, the Lord spoke a word to me during a worship service at my church. I heard Him say, "You are my battle axe!" Then He showed me a vision of a large, well-built warrior wielding a huge axe, cutting down what looked like tall, brown, dried grass or reeds. This was such a heavy word, and I did not take it lightly. I did not share it with anyone at first because I was seeking the Lord to see if this was a word for me, for the body, or both. I do this with any and every word of the Lord that I hear. Proper direction, timing, and appropriation of the Word of the Lord are key factors to seeing the word fulfilled in our lives. It's vital that we seek Him for further instructions after receiving any Word.

The more I meditated on the battle axe, the more I wanted insight. I did some research on the internet and found a wonderful article that really spoke to my heart and brought clarity. I did not want to go by my interpretation alone, so I decided to call on some ministry friends. I sent out an email to my prophet friends to see if I could get a consensus on the scripture and the vision I saw. I received various responses, most of which confirmed what the Lord had been speaking to my heart.

In essence, I knew that it was going to be a year of warfare and victory, in that order. I knew that the Father was positioning me to be one that goes to battle with the enemy. There would be literal and spiritual battles over souls, fears, hurts and territories. Although victory was imminent, I knew that every battle was going to be intense.

When God speaks a word to us, we don't always know the full ramifications of that word. Many times, we don't even feel like that word is being fulfilled in our lives. I was having one of those days when I asked the Lord, "What's up?!" I surely didn't feel like a battle axe; I felt more like a used piece of wood. However, when I awoke the next morning, I was amazed at the difference a day makes, especially in our spirits. The word is true when it says that we have new mercies every morning. (Lamentations 3:22-23) I felt like I was ready to take on the enemies of the kingdom single handedly (not really, but you get my point). No offense meant here, but we can truly be silly sheep at times. One day we are under the dirt of the earth in defeat, and the next we are on the mountain top banging our chest saying, "Bring it on!" Maybe it's just me. Maybe I am the only one that has flip-flop days at times.

The truth of the matter is that the Word of God is consistent and true in our lives, not because of us, but because He said it. The heavens and earth are still in existence today because of a word He spoke. You're breathing air right now because of a word He spoke before man existed. Take a minute and read Genesis chapter one and selah at the marvelous works of our God. Then, I want you to tell me why. Why do we fret? Why do we worry? Why?

If His Word is still standing today, then you better know that any word that He has spoken in your life is yet alive. I'm preaching to myself even if you don't catch it! If He says that I'm a battle axe, it doesn't matter if I feel like it at the moment or not. My feelings have nothing to do with it being true and it being yet alive and working in my life. My existence, my function and my gifts are not governed by tangible circumstances – money, status, position, or the lack thereof. All that I am is governed by my supernatural, eternal relationship with my heavenly Father and the word that He has spoken.

Tomorrow you may feel like I felt: tired, discouraged, and powerless. You may even feel that way now, but I want to encourage your heart. I want you to keep these two things in mind today and in the days ahead. First, know that *"weeping may endure for a night, but joy cometh in the morning." (Psalms 30:5)* Secondly, know that the Word of God, whether spoken or written, is alive and that it will accomplish all that the Father set it out to accomplish.

"For as the rain cometh down, and the snow from heaven, and returneth not thither, but watereth the earth, and maketh it bring forth and bud, that it may give seed to the sower, and bread to the eater: So shall my word be that goeth forth out of my mouth: it shall

not return unto me void, but it shall accomplish that which I please, and it shall prosper in the thing whereto I sent it." ~Isaiah 55:10-11 KJV

    Be encouraged and know that you will see the fulfillment of His promises in your life! **Having done all to stand, stand therefore. (Ephesians 6:13-14)** Stand in agreement with your heavenly Father. Today, I am choosing to stand in agreement with my Father. I am His battle axe. I am taking back territory, souls, removing hurts, and breaking the chains of bondage all for the sake of the kingdom of God. It's not because I am all that, but because He is! I am who He says I am, and His Word is being fulfilled in my life. Hallelujah!

Police Woman

"Thou art my battle axe and weapons of war: for with thee will I break in pieces the nations, and with thee will I destroy kingdoms."
~ Jeremiah 51:20 KJV

When I was a little girl my family used to call me "Police Woman." Stop laughing right now! I can hear all of you. They called me that because I was always bringing attention and correction to the "bad" things that were going on around the house. If my brothers, nephews, or nieces were doing something they weren't supposed to be doing, I was going to make sure my momma knew it and they did too. This "policing" that I did caused conflict with my family, sometimes leading to small acts of violence. As a young girl, I didn't get it. I couldn't understand why my family members would get so upset. They knew what they were doing was wrong, right? I was simply trying to be a help and point it out for them just in case they were not aware (smile). Just call me the Defender of Justice if you will. I was always trying to keep everyone on the straight and narrow. Oh, how I needed to be adjusted and trained. Thank You, Holy Spirit!

My "policing" probably would not have been unusual if I was the oldest, or even second oldest. Most parents expect the eldest children to take some leadership type responsibility in the family at some point. Well, at least I do. In hindsight, I think the real issue for most of my family, and rightly so, wasn't in the fact that I was shining a light on their issues. Rather, they were upset because their younger sister was pointing out their problems. You see, I am number twelve of thirteen siblings: ten boys and three girls. Yes, my Mom is a phenomenal woman! (Love you, Mom!)

Praise be to God for His grace and mercy! I have since learned that although my heart was noble, my means were all wrong. Since that time,

I have also come to realize that this Defender of Justice attitude in me, although a nuisance to the family, was a part of the gifting that the Father placed in me. Of course, it needed to be submitted and governed by the Holy Spirit. I will be honest with you. There were times in my years of growing into a place of maturity that I felt like this "gift" was a curse. I no longer wanted to be the Defender of Justice. In time, I became weary of its qualities and sometimes consequences. I didn't want to see what I saw and know what I knew. I just wanted to blend in with the crowd. You know, *"Que Sera, Sera!"*

Like King David, I cried out to the Lord in my distress saying, "Why, O Lord, do I have to see the stuff I see? Why can't I just be oblivious to all that's going on around me and just enjoy being alive? Why do I even care what my neighbor is doing?" The Holy Spirit quickly convicted my spirit on that kind of thinking and reminded me not to take on the attitude of Cain. **"Am I my brother's keeper?" (Genesis 4:9)** Cain had the wrong mindset which led to the wrong attitude which led to the wrong actions.

Oftentimes, I have tried to close my spiritual eyes and pretend like I can't see anything. *Now you know that doesn't work, right?!* I would be in places or services where, to the natural eye, everyone and everything seems to be okay. Yet, my spirit was so vexed from the spiritual warfare that was going on in the atmosphere that I just wanted to find a closet so that I could war in prayer. Yea, it used to sound a little crazy to me too, but this is who God has called me to be!

Sometimes I don't get this being He has created called me. In all my revelation and discovery there are still times when I look at myself in a mirror and say, "Who are you?" Those times of self-evaluation seem to center around those moments of intense spiritual attacks and warfare. And although I'm not unfamiliar with spiritual warfare, it is still that -- warfare. Spiritual warfare has a way of making you feel inadequate. The constant battles in the spirit, and sometimes even in the natural, can be very stressful, creating a yoke upon you that is not from God.

The Lord says in His word that, **"His yoke is easy and His burdens are light." (Matthew 11:30)** Notice that He did not say that there would be no yoke. He said that His yoke is easy, but there is a yoke. I want to encourage you to seek Him in times of heaviness. When I feel a situation weighing on me (as a yoke), the first thing that I do is ask the Lord, "Is this yoke from You?" If it's from Him, then I know that He has already made the provision of grace for me to carry it and that it is not meant to destroy me but rather to build me. If it's not, then I know to pray for that yoke to be removed.

There has been a surge of acceleration in my life. Good things. Many opportunities for ministry are being laid at my feet and the Lord is opening doors in ways that I know could only be Him. However, along with this surge and acceleration toward the things of God there has also been a surge and acceleration in spiritual attacks and warfare. It seems that I must contend with issues and situations on a regular basis. Warfare has increased in this season and has pushed me to a place, once again, of examining my heart.

When things are such as they are now, I find myself on my face a whole lot crying out to the Lord. I go into my prayer closet because I want Him to examine my heart. I want Him to make adjustments in my spirit. I want Him to bring clarity and give direction, a proper course of action to the situations at hand. And many times, I boldly rush into His presence, wanting Him to bring comfort and strength to my weary spirit. It is in these times of warfare and evaluation that the Father reminds me of my frame, my makeup. He reminds me of who He has called me to be and what He has called me to do. It's in these times that He brings clarity and direction for the next step He desires me to take and He shows me just how much He loves me through the comfort of His word, both written and spoken.

I am thankful to the Lord for this time of acceleration, growth, and warfare. He said to me, **"But my horn you have exalted like a wild ox; I have been anointed with fresh oil." (Psalms 92:10)** He also reminded of what I have been called to do in this season and the scripture He gave me: **"Thou art my battle axe and weapons of war: for with thee will I break in pieces the nations, and with thee will I destroy kingdoms." (Jeremiah 51:20)** Yesteryear, I was a little girl that my family called "Police Woman." Today, I am the righteousness of God in Christ Jesus and the Father calls me His "Battle Axe." Hallelujah!

I pray that during your adversity you find rest and peace in Him and who He has called you to be. Rest in knowing that He is omniscience (all knowing), omnipresent (all present), and omnipotent (all powerful). Is there anything too hard for Him?! *SELAH.*

Leading by Following

"Be ye followers of me, even as I also am of Christ."
~ I Corinthians 11:1 KJV

I am a dance instructor and have been officially teaching dance for about twenty years now. I spend most of my time working on curriculum and class objectives for the classes that I teach. I am also a dance choreographer. I listen and coordinate movement to music in hopes of creating a tapestry of movement that will touch the heart. Although I have choreographed to secular music, my heartbeat is worship. Many, probably most, of the pieces that I have done over the years are with Christian songs. I really enjoy teaching and choreographing and love to see the impact that it makes on the lives of others.

The only problem with teaching and choreographing all the time is that I am always on the other side of learning. It is not often that I get a chance to follow someone else's dance steps. And when I am privileged to do so it's a challenge to my brain. I must consciously come out of teacher mode, wanting to instruct and adjust, and make an intentional effort to follow.

When my friend, Michelle, was working on an African American program, I had the opportunity to dance with her for the finale dance piece. It was a rare occasion for me to learn someone else's choreography. Because of the nature of the program, the dance style was, of course, African, or at least greatly influenced by it. I knew then that it was going to be a challenge, but I was up to it. My dance background is ballet, ballet, a little modern and jazz, and ballet. Asking me to do African-style dancing is like asking Barbara Streisand to do a Mary J. Blige song or vice versa. They could probably pull it off because of their level of skill, but the distinction of their different styles would stand out. Don't get me wrong. It's not that I could not dance an African style; I have danced many styles over the years. My concern was what I would look like dancing it. Whenever I pictured myself dancing to the African music, I would shake my head and laugh.

Michelle confessed early on that she was not the greatest instructor. I soon found that to be untrue. She quickly explained the scenario of the dance and started taking me through the dance movements. I was doing my best to imitate what she demonstrated while at the same time trying to find the rhythm and count of the music. I stumbled over movements for about the first twenty minutes, but soon found my flow. I was able to learn the dance in one night. Praise God! Being at that rehearsal and having to follow and learn the new dance moves made me think about my role as leader and follower. The whole time that I was learning the dance, I thought to myself, "I need to do this more often." Follow, that is.

When you're leading all the time, sometimes you can forget what it's like to have to follow. When I stepped outside of my comfort zone for the African dance, it made me reevaluate my leadership abilities. It made me think of the dancers I oversee at my church and whether I was demonstrating Godly leadership before them. It put me in remembrance of the word and reminded me that I needed to walk even more in the Fruit of the Spirit. (Galatians 5:22-23) I needed to be more patient, kind, understanding, and gentle, not only with them, but with my family as well. It reminded me that if I would just trust the instruction of my leaders that eventually I would produce a beautiful tapestry of life and movement. Finally, it reminded me that to be a good leader you must be a great follower.

Our Lord and Savior, Jesus Christ, is a great leader. He is the good Shepherd: ***"I am the good shepherd. (John 10:11) But thou, O Lord, art a God full of compassion, and gracious, long suffering, and plenteous in mercy and truth." (Psalm 86:15)*** As followers of Christ, we can be assured that if we put our trust in Him and are obedient to His word that our lives will be a beautiful tapestry before Him and man.

My prayer today is that I would be a good leader in whatever capacity the Father places me in, but more than that, a good follower. I want to lead with integrity and love and follow with humility and obedience. I want to honor God as well as the godly men and women He placed as a spiritual covering for my life. May my life and yours be an example of Him today.

Say Yes!

"Now the word of the Lord came to Jonah the son of Amittai, saying, 'Arise, go to Nineveh, that great city, and cry out against it; for their wickedness has come up before Me. But Jonah arose to flee to Tarshish from the presence of the Lord. He went down to Joppa, and found a ship going to Tarshish; so he paid the fare, and went down into it, to go with them to Tarshish from the presence of the Lord.'" ~Jonah 1:1-3 NKJV

As a little girl, I thought Jonah was a great story. But of course, Jonah's journey was more than a great children's story. The prophet of God living inside a whale for three days after being swallowed by a giant whale is an amazing story for people of any age. When examined a little deeper, you find that it is a story of the mercy and forgiveness of a loving Father. A Father who, rather than destroy a sinful and undeserving people, decided to send a message of hope and redemption. What a beautiful description and display of the Father's love toward us. There is nothing He would not do to redeem man unto himself. He displayed this love to the greatest degree when He sent His son, Jesus, to die for our sins. O, What love He has for us!

Yes, Jonah was a great story of love, but there is another side of the story that I believe we can relate to all too often -- saying *no* to God. Jonah is one of the rare stories in the Bible where the featured character is in rebellion against the Lord. It is a story of a man, a prophet, who rebelled against the instructions of the Lord. He basically told God, "No, I'm not going to do it," and then tried to go the other direction. I chuckle every time I think about it. Listen, for a "yes and amen" girl that's a big deal. How in the world does anyone, especially a prophet, say no to God?

Even worse, how does one try to run away from His presence? It sounds ridiculous *and* funny, doesn't it?! Yet, I must admit that, unfortunately, I have found myself with that same attitude as Jonah. It's sad, but true. In fact, there have been times where I found myself resisting something that I heard Him speak to my spirit. Although I didn't try to run from His presence, I did try to avoid the words He spoke. You know the Holy Spirit wasn't having it though! I was confronted and my heart repented and that is my hope for you if you find yourself in a similar situation.

Now, I know you may be thinking, "Shame on you, Dorothy!" or saying, "What!? Not, Dorothy!" or even sighing, "Girl, I know just how you feel." No matter your position or commentary on the matter, the fact is, just like Jonah's, my attitude was all wrong. As much as I wanted to buck against and run away from what I heard the Lord saying, my spirit man (the true me) knew that I must, eventually, surrender. You see, like Jonah, I cannot deny that I hear the voice of the Lord. I believe, and have come to know, that I am a mouthpiece for Him and that He speaks to my heart. Often my response is, "Yes, Lord." or "I hear you Father." When specific instructions are given, I respond, "I will take care of it." However, there are times that the Lord speaks and because of my issues (we *all* have them), I resist His direction and instruction.

One of the fascinating things in the story of Jonah is the fact that the initial reason that Jonah resisted is because I believe he didn't understand the Father's heart. He was so consumed with his opinions, his thoughts, his ideas, and his perspective, that he couldn't see what the Father saw -- a broken people, consumed in sin and in need of a savior. Jonah couldn't understand in his finite thinking how the Father could love the ungodly and sinful people of Nineveh. How could God love idol worshippers, sex offenders, thieves, prostitutes, and countless other unspeakable things? Jonah couldn't understand how His holy God could even want to redeem such a people to Himself. Jonah's actions clearly showed that in all his loyalty in serving God, he missed the very essence of Him. He overlooked His unfailing love for the people He created. He missed the fact that the Father desired from the beginning of time for man to be in fellowship with Him. Genesis shows us that the Father enjoyed fellowshipping with His people, and He was saddened when sin entered the picture and broke that communion. He missed the fact that since that time God has desired to redeem man back unto Himself. He missed the fact that the Father's love saw past the sins of Nineveh and saw a people in need of Him. Jonah just didn't get it and oftentimes I (we) don't get it either.

Our lives, our gifts, our talents, our abilities were never about us, but rather to fulfill His purposes on earth! He chose Jonah to be a mouthpiece that would send a word and set the people free. Instead of Jonah seeing the mercy and love of the Father, he sat in his pride and resisted. "Let the people die in their sins," was Jonah's thought. He just decided to override the Lord's decision to give the people the opportunity to be redeemed. How arrogant of him! What pride! What a shame, right? And yet, I have found myself being stuck in that same pride overriding God's decisions of mercy and grace by telling God, *no*. Wow. SELAH.

I don't know about you, but my lips and my heart repents to My Father even now. *Who are we to ever think that we know better than You, my Lord? Forgive us. Forgive me.*

Yes, the Father will ask you and I to say or do things that we may not want to at times. But it is at those times that we must humble ourselves, break the spirit of pride, and open our hearts and spiritual eyes to see the greater purpose; we must see His heart. It is not about us. God is not always concerned with our comfort. He's more concerned with the condition of man's heart. It's all about Him and redeeming people unto Him.

The next time the Father speaks to your heart and asks you to do something that you may not want to do and you find yourself resisting what the Lord is saying to you, ask yourself these questions:

--Did I hear the Lord clearly? What instructions did He give me? **"My sheep hear my voice, and I know them, and they follow me." (John 10:27)**

--Why am I resisting Him, not wanting to obey? Is it fear, pride, personal opinion, self-righteousness, envy, jealousy, etc.? **"Let us lay aside every weight, and the sin which doth so easily beset us, and let us run with patience the race that is set before us..." (Hebrews 12:1)**

--Ask the Holy Spirit to open your spiritual eyes to the greater purpose. Ask Him to help you see beyond the natural. **"The eyes of your understanding being enlightened; that ye may know what is the hope of his calling, and what the riches of the glory of his inheritance in the saints..." (Ephesians 1:18)**

--Ask the Father to humble your heart and give you the grace to walk in obedience. ***"Wherefore he saith, God resisteth the proud, but giveth grace unto the humble." (James 4:6)***

Today I say, "Yes!" Yes, to my Father. Yes, to His will. Yes, to His way. Yes, to His purposes. Yes, to His plans. I don't always understand why He does what He does, but I trust that it's rooted in His unfailing love for you and for me. I choose today to be a willing vessel; what about you? Will you say, "Yes!" today?

Embracing Who I Am

"For we are his workmanship, created in Christ Jesus unto good works, which God hath before ordained that we should walk in them."
~Ephesians 2:10 KJV

Over the years I've taken dozens of personality tests. You know the ones that tell you if you're a high D, low C, average B. *I'm being facetious.* I personally think that every person should take one at least once in their life. My husband and I were privileged to take one that was developed from a biblical perspective. It was a wonderful experience and really brought light to some common traits and trends in our lives.

In all the tests that I've taken, the one thing that has always surfaced to the top is my ability to be a strong leader: organized, administrative, passionate, etc. Now add to that a leaning toward the prophetic and apostolic, and man, that's a doozy of a mix. These are great traits to have, but they can be a bit much, not always rubbing people the right way. It seems, at times, that I am always apologizing to someone for being too straight or harsh. The Holy Spirit, my Paraclete, is always right there checking me, saying, "Right song, wrong melody." My poor husband and family suffers the brunt of it all. Praise God for mercy and grace.

Don't get me wrong, I am not ragging on my personality because it's not all bad. The same passion that is God-given to lead, also goes very deep giving me a love for God and His people that's hard to shake. This deep love is sometimes reflected in correction, protection, and confrontation. At times, it even causes me to feel the pain and anguish of others, compelling me to aggressively confront the enemies of God on their behalf.

The Lord has confirmed His heart for my life many times often showing me myself in the Word of God. He gives me scriptures or points to Bible characters that show similar personality traits. At one time or another, He has told me that I was like the Apostle Paul, John the Baptist, Huldah, Esther, and a few others. And of course, there's that Battle Axe! (Jeremiah 51:20)

Don't misunderstand. I am not saying that I have the exact personality traits as these Bible saints. I believe that the Father pointed to these men and women of God to show how I function in the earth. There are times when I must establish, uproot, correct, and speak truth like Apostle Paul. There are times when I warn, expose, and compel others (even myself) to repentance like John the Baptist. Then there are times when the Lord requires me to be ready with a Word of the Lord, as Huldah was for King Josiah. And there are times that I must walk in the beauty and favor of the Lord, using strategy and wisdom to overcome the enemy as Esther did to save her nation. And once the Lord paralleled my life with that of a Battle Axe, the warfare has been nonstop!

I've learned to embrace these special traits but to be honest with you, I have often wondered, "Lord, why did you make me this way? Why can't I be the little, quiet wife next door with the meek and mild spirit? Whyyyy, do I have to be the loud and pushy one, making my opinion known in one way or the other?" I must work overtime to make sure that I am always operating in the Fruit of the Spirit (Galatians 5:22). One slip and there can be serious damage. Yes! The Lord is working on a sistah, teaching and reminding her every day to submit those "traits" under the guidance of the Holy Spirit. I am a work in progress.

I don't always like having to be who I am called to be; sometimes I am like the Toys 'R Us kids - "I don't wanna grow up..." But over the years, the Lord has broken my spirit (in a good way) and has revealed to me the secret of walking in my calling, in His power, and authority. The secret is in the arms of the Father. Even Jesus himself, who had no doubt of who He was and what He was called to do in the earth, knew where to go to find strength for journey. It was in prayer and in the presence of the Father. Jesus understood this concept and often spent time in prayer. I won't take the time or space to go into it but when you have a chance, look up in a Bible concordance how many times it is said that Jesus went up to pray, or off to pray, or they found Him praying. You will be amazed. Like Jesus, I have learned to find comfort and peace in the presence of the Lord. It is in His presence that I can take off my armor. I love who I am and what He has called me to be, but what I love more is Him.

This prophetic, apostolic, warrior-type girl will take on the enemy any day, anytime, but know this - I run to the arms of my Father every day. I await His embrace, His love, His tenderness, and mercy. In His arms, I am restored. In His arms, I am comforted. It is His Love that compels me to once again embrace the traits that He has bestowed upon me. It is His Love that compels me to be strong and courageous yet another day. It is knowing that the Father's arms are open and outstretched to me that gives me strength for the day.

My prayer today is that you will embrace all that the Father has called you to be. I pray that the Holy Spirit will bring revelation and illumination of the Word so that you can see who you are in Christ Jesus. I pray that the Father will show you traits in Bible characters that are like yours and that you begin to nurture those traits through the Holy Spirit. And finally, I pray that when all is said and done that you will run to His outstretched arms and allow Him to love on you, as only He can.

Give Me a Clean Heart

"Create in me a clean heart..." ~Psalm 51:10 KJV

Recently, I felt such a need in my spirit to set aside a time of consecration to the Lord, taking some time for fasting and prayer. My plate was quickly filling, and I could see all the business and ministry responsibilities coming my way. I could sense the Lord encouraging me to prepare my heart. It's a necessity that I'm able to hear the Holy Spirit clearly and follow His leading. I know that that clarity and desire to hear His voice even more only comes through spending time before the Lord in prayer and fasting.

Like every other believer, I desire my spirit man to line up with the desires of the Lord. I, too, want to be a vessel that He works through. At the same time, I want to be a pure vessel, one that is sensitive and led by the Lord. I don't want to operate in my flesh, my own strength which, believe it or not, is so easy to do. Even when doing good things, it's easy to look up and you're no longer being led by the Spirit, but rather are operating in your strengths.

That's why I believe that it is so critical that we, as believers, learn how to hear and remain sensitive to the voice of the Holy Spirit and follow His leading. I believe that it is critical that we learn to be in sync with Him. I believe that this is one of the many safeguards that God the Father put in place to help us. I don't have time to go into it today, but there are so many examples in scripture that show that God hates when we put our trust in our own strengths. The Lord desires that He would be our source. We should purpose to walk with the Spirit daily, allowing Him to be our guide in all things.

"This I say then, walk in the Spirit, and ye shall not fulfill the lust of the flesh." ~Galatians 5:16 KJV

My prayer today, and always, is that the Father God would continue to purify and cleanse my heart so that I can minister out of a pure vessel. I want to fully rely on His power and His strength and not my own. I want to be led by Him and Him alone, purposing to daily decrease as He increases in me. (John 3:30)

I want to encourage you to always seek Him first in all things. Purpose to never get to a place where you don't need the Lord, being confident in your own strength. Purpose to minister out of a pure heart, not giving your own opinions and counsel solely based on your knowledge and intellect. Earnestly pray that through the leading of the Spirit you can speak (or whatever He asks you to do) that which the Lord desires to be heard. Your greatest desire should be pleasing the Lord first, your audience of One.

Consistency of Character

"If it be so, our God whom we serve is able to deliver us from the burning fiery furnace, and he will deliver us out of thine hand, O king. But if not, be it known unto thee, O king, that we will not serve thy gods, nor worship the golden image which thou hast set up."
~Daniel 3:17-18 KJV

Several years ago, I was blessed to be able to hear the spoken word of Dr. Jack Hayford. Prior to hearing him speak, I was not that knowledgeable of his ministry, but I knew he was a pioneer and giant in the kingdom. Dr. Hayford did not disappoint; his words left me reflecting for days, months and since I am writing about it now--even years later. There were many things that were said that seemed to hit me right in the heart, but one statement stuck with me. Dr. Hayford described the fruits of the anointing. He went on to say how people are able to recognize this anointing through one of three ways: 1) Through the demonstration of the Holy Spirit with power (seeing the healing, deliverance, and power of the spirit working through you) 2) Through the demonstration of consistency of character in the difficult times 3) Through the submission of your heart before God (allowing God to make a place for you rather than vying for yourself) These are three powerful manifestations of the anointing. I could instantly see God working all three demonstrations in my life, but for some reason that 'Consistency of Character' just kept ringing in my spirit.

As 'Consistency of Character' rang in my spirit, the Holy Spirit asked me a question. He said, "If life never changes for you, and you remain where you are indefinitely, are you willing to live a life that is consistent toward Me?" On the surface, that would seem like an easy question to answer. I could have easily said, "Yes, Lord!" I have been walking with the Lord a long time, so I knew that it was more to the question than the obvious. I knew that the Father didn't ask that question without a purpose. My girlfriend had a plaque in her kitchen that read, "Advice is what we ask for when we already know the answer." Of course, God doesn't need advice, but one thing I'm sure of is that He already knew the answer to the question He had just put before me. Then you ask, "So, why the question?" I'll tell you why--to reveal deep the recesses of my heart.

It seemed that time suspended forever, although it was only thirty seconds, as I pondered and contemplated the question. I could hear my heart saying, "Whoa! Wait a minute! What do you mean, if?" Suddenly "if" became the biggest word in the dictionary. I begin to think about where I was, what I had been through, what I was going through, what was before, and what was to come. You see, I can't be fake with the Father. You can't hide what's in your heart. He is omniscient: all knowing.

Anybody can say they have faith when there is an expected end to their situation, but what if there is none? Think about that. What if your situation never changes? Are you still able to stand and still able to say, "I trust Him"? Are you able to trust that He knows what's best for you? Are you walking out Ephesians and having done all to stand, still standing? You see, many times we think we are walking in faith in God, but we are walking in the things that we want from Him. There is a difference.

The Father was again challenging my faith and revealing my heart. (Ouch!) Was I walking in faith for better things? Was I walking in faith for change only? Was I walking in faith to see me set free from the heavy cares of this life? Or was I really putting my faith in Him, totally trusting Him to orchestrate my life whatsoever way He chooses? Was I walking in the same faith as Shadrach, Meshach, and Abed-Nego, whose hearts were just sold out to Him whether He came through for them or not?

"If it be so, our God whom we serve is able to deliver us from the burning fiery furnace, and he will deliver us out of thine hand, O king. But if not, be it known unto thee, O king, that we will not serve thy gods, nor worship the golden image which thou hast set up." ~Daniel 3:17-18 KJV

Understand that your faith must live between Daniel 3:17-18: He IS able, He WILL deliver, BUT IF NOT. Your faith must be in God, trusting that He can deliver. Yet, that same faith, if it's truly in Him, will not wane even if He doesn't deliver. We must be careful as believers to not allow our faith to be misdirected. You can have faith in self, wealth, people, circumstances, well-wishers (flatterers), jobs, friends, churches, and even pastors. Any faith that is not totally in Jesus, and Him alone, is misdirected faith.

Faith in Him, although our first responsibility as believers, does not dictate God's actions. He is God and squares by no one but himself and He cannot be manipulated in any kind of way. However, our faith in God moves His heart. It's our faith in Him that accounts towards us salvation, as it did with Abraham. (Romans 4:1-5) Our faith and trust in Him speaks of our relationship with Jesus. And by His faithfulness, He will manifest His promises and even our desires, not based on our actions, but based upon His love for us.

I love what Dr. Hayford, a man with the gentle spirit of the Lord, said: "I believe in impartation. I believe in the laying on of hands. But it is up to the Father, after I have laid hands, to determine if and what is to be imparted and to what measure." (paraphrased) Those were such words of wisdom from the man of God. We hold no power in and of ourselves. As we act in faith, the power of God can be translated through us. To the natural mind it doesn't make sense, but when you know the true realm in which we live it makes perfect sense.

So, what was my answer to the Lord? Well, you know... Of course, I said to Him, "Yes, Lord! My heart is yours and as painful and uncomfortable as it would be to my flesh, I am willing to live this life as You dictate. Because I love you more." I truly want to live like Shadrach, Meshach, Abed-Nego, Esther, John the Baptist, and Paul. I want to live a life poured out for Him, not with all the bells and whistles that come from man's success. I want to live the life that He has personally chosen and destined for me. I know that may mean that sometimes life will not be pretty to the natural eye. However, if there is beauty in the spirit by my life of obedience to Him, and if I know that He is pleased then I know I have fulfilled my purpose in the earth.

My declaration: I am purposing to be 'Consistent in Character' in difficult times that I might please my Father and display His anointing.

Impact

"Let your light so shine before men, that they may see your good works, and glorify your Father which is in heaven."
~ Matthew 5:16 KJV

m-pakt – 1: to have a direct effect or impact on: impinge on 2: to strike forcefully; also: to cause to strike forcefully.

Impact. That's the word that I heard ringing in my spirit as I was thinking about and praying over my natural and spiritual sisters and daughters. As I was calling out the many urgent needs of each one to the Father, my heart ached for them. I wanted to be superwoman and jump in and fix all the problems, including my own, with my magic power. Of course, I knew that wasn't possible. So, I acquiesced and continued to call out and rely on my main source of power, which is prayer.

Intercession is my weapon of war and I purpose to stay armed with it at all times so that I can drive back the forces of hell and darkness that try to overtake my sisters and brothers and even myself. I know that we wrestle not against flesh and blood. And I know that the weapons of our warfare, what we use to fight, are not carnal (fleshly). The Bible says that the weapons that we do have, prayer being one of them, are MIGHTY through God to the point of pulling down strongholds. Needless to say, I believe in the power of prayer.

"For though we walk in the flesh, we do not war after the flesh: (For the weapons of our warfare are not carnal, but mighty through God to the pulling down of strong holds;) ~2 Corinthians 10:3-4 KJV

Yet, there are times when I feel as if I am not doing enough, even though I pray diligently. I feel that I am not striking forcefully enough, as the definition of 'impact' says. In times like that, I feel most helpless. When I feel the weightiness of those I care about so much, when the needs are so great, and I sense the heaviness in the hearts of many of my daughters, I wish I could do or say more that would bring change. Change in perspective, change in action, change in their level of faith, change in those around them, change in attitude, and even change in direction.

It's in those times that I want to have the kind of Godly impact, through word and deed, that will bring transformation to the lives of those who are in my circle of influence. Although I believe that I am having *some* impact, I want to have the impact that, as the definition said, causes others to strike forcefully. Impact that moves my sisters and daughters to action in the natural and in the spirit. Maybe that's just the prophetic, black and white warrior in me. I don't know. I just believe that true impact is shown by the actions that follow. If we say we are followers of Christ, then shouldn't our lives reflect through actions our relationship and love for Him?

I pray that I am really making a difference in the lives of those He has graciously allowed to be in my circle of influence. Sometimes, I worry and question myself. *Am I really making an impact?* I don't want to just be a crutch for others to lean on. I want to be the one that administers the healing balm of Jesus so that others can walk on their own. I want to have that godly impact that causes others to also have a godly impact. I want my life to reflect Jesus and impact everything and everyone around me, not for my own glory, but that the Father may be glorified.

I am reminded of a song that I was asked to sing many years ago: "Praise You" by Brooklyn Tabernacle Choir. At that time, the minister of music and his team would pray over songs and assign the soloist as the Holy Spirit led. They wanted the songs to be ministered, not necessarily by the best singers (I was not one of them), but by the heart cry of the worshipper. When I was approached with the song, I really didn't want to do it. I was scared and very insecure in my abilities as a lead singer. Of course, I ended up singing the song and the impact that it had on all those who heard it is still resonating today. Even when I revisit the church years later, it is always requested that I sing that song. I don't believe it's because I sing it so well; as a matter of fact, I know it's not for that reason. It's because it's truly the cry and prayer of my heart.

I pray as you listen to the lyrics of that song or another that the Lord lays on your heart, that it will become your prayer unto the Lord as well. Praying today for all my natural and spiritual sisters, daughters, and brothers too. I am praying that my life, and your life, will have godly impact on every circumstance and all those around you and me. In Jesus' Name. Amen!

On Mondays

"Trust in the LORD with all thine heart; and lean not unto thine own understanding. In all thy ways acknowledge him, and he shall direct thy paths. Be not wise in thine own eyes: fear the LORD, and depart from evil. It shall be health to thy navel, and marrow to thy bones."
~Proverbs 3:5-8 KJV

Those who are close to me know that Mondays are my marathon day. I start early and end late. And although I'm not a "Monday-hater," Monday is the day that puts reality in my face -- the Good, the Bad, and the Ugly. It's on Mondays that I'm reminded that I have deadlines, bills due, and family who needs me. It's on Mondays that I must look forward not back. It's on Mondays that difficult decisions are made that set the tone for the rest of the week.

It's on Mondays that I'm reminded that I'm a wife, covenanted to love and respect my husband. It's on Mondays that I'm reminded that I'm a mother and grandmother that has children who need nurturing, love, and daily encouragement. It's on Mondays that I'm reminded that I am a business owner, purposing to walk in integrity in her finances and toward her clients. It's on Mondays that I'm reminded that I am a leader, privileged and commissioned to intercede, impart, and train other wonderful men and women of God.

It's on Mondays that I'm pressed for time, knowing that I have one more part to choreograph on that dance before the evening's rehearsal. It's on Mondays that I'm reminded that I must project and plan for future events that concern me, my family, ministry, and business.

On Mondays, I realize how vital it is that I spend time in the Word of God and communing with my heavenly Father. It's on Mondays that I seek Him early and linger with Him late into the evening. It's on Mondays that I must be quick to hear the voice of the Holy Spirit speaking to me to guide, to give wisdom and keen discernment. It's on Mondays that I pull and rely on the supernatural grace of the Father to be and do all that He has called me to do.

    On Mondays, I realize that Mondays are every day of my week! I admonish you this Monday or Tuesday or any day of the week ending in "-day" to take a minute to seek Him.

Let It Go!

"Remember ye not the former things, neither consider the things of old. Behold, I will do a new thing; now it shall spring forth; shall ye not know it? I will even make a way in the wilderness, and rivers in the desert." ~Isaiah 43:18-19 KJV

My husband worked in corporate America for twenty-four years. All my children and I knew were blue suits, white shirts, and red ties so to speak. Then years ago, all of that changed. His company, IBM became AT&T and let go of about 1,500 people, many of which had spent their careers at IBM. My husband was one of those people. It was a difficult time for my family. We had one college student, three high-schoolers, and two home-schooled boys. It was a serious adjustment to say the least. The mental adjustment was sometimes harder than the financial adjustment. We did all the things that we could to survive and keep our family afloat, hoping that it would be temporary, and my husband would soon be back in corporate America doing what he did. Well, one month passed, three months passed, one year passed and...nothing. It seemed that life as we knew it was never to be again.

At first, I had a hissy fit over the situation. I literally went through the five stages of grief. I can laugh about it now, but there were many tears then. It was rough. I wanted things to be back to normal. I wanted *my* life back. I wanted to be comfortable. I didn't want to adjust. I didn't want things to change. I didn't want to shift. I didn't want to move forward. I was stuck -- stuck in what was, stuck in the past. I couldn't see beyond it. I couldn't see any good at that time. I think I went through the grieving process at least three times before I got to the point of acceptance. My life as I knew it changed forever, never to be the same again. And you know, that was the best place that I could have ever been.

No, things were not great. We were struggling financially and working hard to recover from that season. Our family went through some even deeper valleys after that time. We were hit hard. Our finances and job situations were not looking any better, but what changed was my attitude. I decided to let it go! I decided to stop trying to relive what was. I decided to accept where I was. That was my new normal. I decided to look to my future, which was an open range when I looked through my spiritual eyes (the better ones). I decided to move forward. We must be careful that we don't allow circumstances, people, and even our missed expectations to change us. No matter what happens around us, we can still fulfill our purpose in life; we can still reach our goals. The key is to let go of what was so that we can embrace what is to be.

It was at that time that I decided that I would take on more dance students. It was at that time that I decided to get up off my bed of "yesterday" and move toward my purpose, which had never changed. It was at that time that I decided that I would try this thing called Zumba and my life changed forever. I never knew I could love fitness as much as I do. After all, I'm a dancer; fitness was not on my menu. But God! The power of letting go is immeasurable.

Whatever you are facing today, don't get stuck! Let it go! We all make mistakes, get off track, and sometimes suffer things that are not even our fault (divorce, financial struggles, sickness, etc.), but it's up to us what we do with it. I want to encourage you to refocus yourself, go through the grief process if you need to, and then get up and move. It's time to be about your purpose. It's time to press toward those goals! It's time to let the past be the past and for you to press into your new normal!

Listen, when you let it go, it only gets better. Trust me on that! I let go of a lot of things a few years back, good and bad. However, I am so glad that I chose to let go, because I would not have had the pleasure of meeting so many of the wonderful people that I know. I wouldn't have had the opportunity to meet the NFL and WNBA players who I have come to love. I wouldn't have had the pleasure of crossing the seas to the Philippines to encounter the loving people there. I wouldn't have the pleasure of sharing how good My God is with you. (Smile) I am so glad that I let go. Despite what my circumstances screamed at me years ago, God is good!

I refuse to be discouraged by circumstances, people, even sometimes by my own missed expectations. Today, I choose to look up. I choose and purpose to keep my mind, heart, and focus on the good things that are ahead, and so should you. Life is too short to dwell on yesterday. If it's not taking you toward your goal or purpose, let it go and move forward! Let it go and move forward!

My Love Song to Him

"Ye are our epistle written in our hearts, known and read of all men: Forasmuch as ye are manifestly declared to be the epistle of Christ ministered by us, written not with ink, but with the Spirit of the living God; not in tables of stone, but in fleshy tables of the heart. And such trust have we through Christ to God-ward: Not that we are sufficient of ourselves to think any thing as of ourselves; but our sufficiency is of God." ~ II Corinthians 3:2-5 KJV

After my husband lost his job in 2007, I was often asked, "How are we doing?" It seemed like a simple question, but I found that I didn't always have a simple answer. Most times, when I heard the question, my brain instantly acted as a computer downloading and cross referencing all the events of my life, past and present. I would hesitate for a moment to think of how to answer the question with honesty without sounding as if I was whining about life. If I were to describe my life, I would have to say that it had been a consistent flow of highs and lows, victories and seemingly defeats, mountain top and valleys. After internally evaluating everything, my answer to most was usually, "We're okay!"

I had not thought anything of that answer but that it was honest. I knew all the things that I was facing. I knew that I could either take the low road, complaining about all that was going wrong or I could take the high road and speak of the victories in my life. Both seemed to be a bit extreme to me and wouldn't give a true picture of where I was…or at least that's how I felt. In the end, being "okay" seemed to be an acceptable answer to most.

I was once explaining to a good friend about how Albert and I were doing. I was trying to create a word picture, describing to her how the victories and struggles seem to simultaneously overlap, not leaving time for us to wallow in defeat or enjoy a victory. Oftentimes, the Holy Spirit will give me pictures in the spirit that help me to grasp or articulate what the Lord is saying. He began to show me wavelengths. At first, I thought that He was speaking of the television airways, but He quickly corrected me. What I was seeing in the spirit was radio wavelengths.

In my mind, I could see several wavelengths in different colors waving and intertwining with each other. Each one of those wavelengths represented a different aspect of my life: marriage, job, children, ministry, and finances. Each wavelength had its highs and lows and were all active at the same time. The Holy Spirit began to give insight as to how my life and my combination of wavelengths made a prophetic "sound" that is exclusive to me. I could see in the spirit the highs and lows and victories and defeats as wavelengths, mixed cohesively to make a melodious sound that is heard in the heavenlies. I believe that "sound" not only goes up before the Father, but it's a "sound" that resonates in the spirit realm. Imagine that, our lives making a "sound." If you can imagine that then you are envisioning a picture of life that I believe is a prophetic declaration.

As I envisioned that picture of wavelengths, I could literally hear the "sound" in the heavenlies. I thought about my signature on all my blogs, *"My Love Song to You."* That signature was taken from a song called "Love Song" by Jason Morant. The song is about our life being a living love song to the Lord and the last chorus speaks of my life being a Love Song to Him. I absolutely love this song; it's so in line with the word of God.

The scripture says that we are "living epistles" read by men (II Corinthians 3:2). What does that mean? It means that we are living books being written, moment by moment, for all the world to see. I believe that the life that we live every day, the choices that we make, and the things that we pursue speak volumes. Our lives are speaking of either Him, us, or the enemy. Which is it for you? What is your life speaking? What are others seeing? What sound are they hearing? Are others seeing Jesus or you? Are they hearing the sound of hope or defeat?

Too often, we live as if we are in a cocoon. We live our lives as if no one can see or hear us. We think that our decisions, good and bad, don't affect anyone but ourselves. We are so deceived. We must learn to discern our lives in the spirit. And let me clear that I'm not speaking of anything "new agey" here. I'm simply making a point that our lives are the vessels that the Father uses to draw others to Him.

Whether we like it or not, we are making a sound in the earth and in the heavens. We can't always control the different "wavelengths" in our lives: children, finances, etc. However, because we belong to Him, we can trust that He will make our lives a glorious melody unto Him. If we submit our lives to Him and embrace His process for our lives, I believe that no matter the highs and lows that what we face, our lives can and will produce a sound that penetrates the heavens and draws men unto Him!

I don't know about you, but I want my life to be a *Love Song* to Him. My prayer is that He will continue to tune and adjust us, so that our lives make a sound that is glorious unto Him, in Jesus' name!

A Mighty Whirlwind

"And there arose a great storm of wind, and the waves beat into the ship, so that it was now full. And he was in the hinder part of the ship, asleep on a pillow: and they awake him, and say unto him, Master, carest thou not that we perish? And he arose, and rebuked the wind, and said unto the sea, Peace, be still. And the wind ceased, and there was a great calm." ~Mark 4:37-39 KJV

In December of 2007, the Lord gave a word to Albert and me as a reminder that He is faithful to what He promised. The word was mainly for my husband, but it spoke to my heart as well. It came at a time when our lives were beginning the pruning process that comes necessary in the life of every believer at some point. If you haven't experienced it yet, you will. Just keep living. Many things were either being cut away or stirred up: jobs, ministry, children, etc. It seemed like our life entered a whirlwind and all was being shaken that could be shaken. The crazy thing is that the Lord warned us that the whirlwind was coming two years prior.

I remembered when I first saw what I thought was a "storm." I had been in prayer and saw in the spirit a huge "storm" coming at me. I remember calling my best girlfriend and describing this huge, dark "storm" and how I was afraid of what it represented. (I kind of knew but didn't want to know.) I was afraid because I could see the "storm" approaching and there was nothing and nobody that could stop it. I was afraid for my flesh which was sure to go through some changes. You know that most of us don't like change. The flesh hates it. We all want to be comfortable, right?! Change was inevitable for us. The "storm" was coming whether I liked it or not. It was not going to leave one stone unturned.

I prayed for weeks about that "storm," talking to the Lord trying to get clarity. And yes, trying to get out of it. Finally, the Lord answered me and took me right to the scriptures. He brought clarity and comfort all at the same time as only He can. You see, it was not a "storm" that I saw, but rather a whirlwind. There is a difference. According to my studies, the whirlwind is a representative of the Lord Himself when mentioned in scriptures. "Wow," is all I could think. The Lord Himself was coming. That changed my whole perspective on things. I was still a little worried, but I was greatly comforted in my spirit because He would be in the midst. I was no longer afraid of what could happen because I knew that it was Him orchestrating the beast of a whirlwind coming at me. I knew that it was going to be rough and painful to my flesh at times. However, knowing that He was in control gave me assurance that all was all going to work for my good. Hallelujah!

Be encouraged and know that God is in the midst of whatever storm you are facing. He is a mighty whirlwind!

What Do You See?

Part I

"Moreover the word of the Lord came to me, saying, "Jeremiah, what do you see?" ~ Jeremiah 1:11 NKJV

I awoke one morning singing and dancing in my spirit. I could literally see myself twirling, jumping, and leaping in the spirit. Of course, I was still lying in bed, but my spirit man was rejoicing. At the time, my family and I were believing the Father for total healing of my youngest daughter, Katheryn. The doctors discovered a growth in her neck that was blocking her air passage; they wanted to go in as soon as possible and remove it. The procedure that they wanted to do could have easily turned into a very invasive surgery so my husband, my children, and a host of other believers stood on the word of God believed that the growth would dissipate, in Jesus' name.

Katheryn had been struggling with her breathing for about three months and I was praying and asking the Father to reveal the real cause. The doctors were saying that her shortness of breath was due to asthma, which I defied from day one. I was very familiar with the symptoms and lifestyle of asthmatics since my husband, my son, and my other daughter all live with it every day. Yet, the doctors thought they knew best and explained to me that people can develop asthma late in life. That may be true, but I was adamant about the fact that she didn't have it. After inhalers, nebulizers, steroids, breath analyzer tests and even an allergy test, my child was still not able to breathe.

Finally, after kind of getting in some faces, we were sent to an ENT (ear, nose & throat) doctor. A CAT scan was ordered, and the growth was revealed. The ENT called Katheryn and I into a consultation to tell us what I was feeling in my gut throughout the whole process of testing and doctor's visits. Surgery was inevitable. That's a word that I didn't want to hear. It brought back all the memories of two years prior when Katheryn had to undergo surgery for Arnold Chiari. It was a major surgery, complete with all the risks and worries but by the grace of God, our family made it through victoriously. All praise to Jesus! Yet, being victorious in one surgery isn't cause to desire another one.

Surgery is not something that I desire to experience, and I surely didn't want my daughter undergoing anything like that again. Yet, there we were, two years later, being given the same options that we were given before. Doing nothing was not an option. We agreed on that fact. However, what we didn't agree on was what to do. They wanted to explore and examine the growth; it's the scientific way. We wanted healing and wholeness without invasive surgery for our daughter; it's the Father's way.

I cried a lot that day. Thinking and praying throughout the rest of the day, I asked the Father for comfort and assurance to my heart. I knew what I needed and desired for my daughter, but I was struggling to find my footing in the spirit. I was so overwhelmed by the thought of surgery, but I knew I needed to refocus, and quickly. I wanted to run home to my prayer closet, my place of security and comfort, but I knew I had responsibilities and obligations that couldn't be changed, so I continued with the cares of the day. By the grace of God, I was able to function (at least partially) and finish the tasks at hand. I was thankful, but honestly, I was longing for the day to be over. I wanted to go to bed and sleep as fast as my body would respond. I wanted the dawning of a new day to come quickly. I wanted and needed to embrace the new mercies of a new day.

When I arrived home around 10:00 that night, I made my way to my bedroom as quickly as possible, bypassing all my usual routines. Through my tears, I spoke with my husband for a few minutes and I was able to find comfort in his words as he reaffirmed our trust in Him. I closed my eyes in peace, the kind that passes all understanding, as I looked forward to receiving clarity and strategy from the Lord. I knew that the Father would make it all clear: where we were, where the enemy was, and where He was. That's all I need is the ability to see, not in the natural, but in the spirit. Seeing for me is everything. It's the way I'm wired by Him and it's how I can war.

What Do You See?

Part II

"So he answered, "Do not fear, for those who are with us are more than those who are with them." And Elisha prayed, and said, "Lord, I pray, open his eyes that he may see." Then the Lord opened the eyes of the young man, and he saw. And behold, the mountain was full of horses and chariots of fire all around Elisha." ~ 2 Kings 6:16-17 NKJV

The new day came, and His mercies were fresh; my spirit man was alive with expectation. I was looking forward to being like Mary that morning, sitting at His feet, eating the good part: ***"But one thing is needful: and Mary hath chosen that good part, which shall not be taken away from her." (Luke 10:42***) The Father was faithful and began to speak to my heart. He asked me, "What do you see?" This was a question He asked me a few years prior.

The Holy Spirit led me to the verse in the first chapter of Jeremiah when the Lord asked the Prophet Jeremiah the same question. Jeremiah's response was, "I see a rod of an almond tree" (Jeremiah 1:11). The Holy Spirit went on to speak to my heart concerning the almond tree (KJV says branch), explaining its meaning (to hasten), and letting me know that He was watching over all that concerned me and was hastening to perform it. It was a word of encouragement to me and Albert that was greatly needed at that time. As I pondered on all that the Lord had spoken to me at that time, for the life of me I could not figure out how it related to my situation at hand.

Well, I learned over the years not to quickly dismiss things when it seems that it's not making sense. I have learned to be patient and wait on the Holy Spirit and allow Him to lead me into all truth. I continued to meditate on the scripture and word the Holy Spirit had given me throughout the day, still not making the connection. Then finally, the next morning, the Spirit of the Lord spoke to me and said, "There be more with you than against you." I was familiar with that Bible story behind that and quickly began to search the scriptures to find it so that I could read in context. And find it, I did.

The word the Holy Spirit had given me was found in 2 Kings 6:8-23. After reading the whole passage, the Holy Spirit spoke to me again and said, "What do you SEE?" Then it hit me! That's the connection. My perception is everything, especially when it comes to spiritual things. Of course, I knew that, but the thought of surgery and the risk involved were so overwhelming that I was shifting my focus. My perspective, my vision and my focus determines my course of direction whether praying, living, dancing, or whatever. I need to be able to "see" in the spirit so that I can walk it out by faith. What I "see" is invisible to the natural, yet it does exist in the spirit. We are to live by faith. (Hebrews 10:38) Faith is not blind or empty. It has substance.

"Now faith is the substance of things hoped for, the evidence of things not seen." ~ Hebrews 11:1 KJV

What I "see" in the spirit is a means to activate my faith at levels that defy the natural. As a matter of fact, the natural realm may be speaking the opposite of what I see in the spirit and you and I must be careful not to allow the natural to dictate our actions or reaction. I often say, "I live in what I see." When I say that, I am speaking from what I see spiritually. I purpose to live life seeing people and perceiving situations as the Spirit of the Lord reveals. The word of God says, *"Where there is no vision, the people perish." (Proverbs 29:18)* Over the years, many have used that as a mantra for building funds and other vision casting avenues in the body of Christ. All of that is well and good. However, I want to challenge you to look at that verse a little differently. I want you to think, "Where there is no [sight, seeing], the people perish."

I believe that the Father desires us to see what He sees. I believe that He desires that we see beyond our situations, our circumstances, our sickness, our financial woes, our marriage problems, and our wayward children. I believe the Lord is challenging His people to live our lives in another realm: to be in the world, but not of the world. He desires that we dwell in the realm where He lives. Where He dwells sickness, disease, hurt, and pain cannot remain. Hallelujah!

The Holy Spirit drew my attention to those passages of scripture in 2 Kings and Jeremiah to remind me to focus my spirit on Him and the realm of the Spirit, not the natural. In the natural, I'm limited by science, by doctors, by finances, and even by people, but in the realm of the spirit there are no limitations.

When we see as the Father sees then fear goes and faith comes. The servant in the passage of scripture in 2 Kings was afraid for himself and for Elisha. Why? He was afraid because he couldn't see what Elisha saw. When the servant came to Elisha in a panic, Elisha didn't beat the man down. Elisha used it as a teaching moment for his servant (and us). Yes, they were surrounded. Yes, there were armed men ready to harm them. Yes, they were without defense against them. Yet, Elisha understood that his servant was missing an element in the current situation. The servant only saw what was visible to the natural eye, so Elisha prayed that the Father would open his spiritual eyes to see the unseen. When the servant's spiritual eyes were opened his perspective changed. Think about that. If we could but only dwell in the things of the spirit, fear and worry would instantly dissipate. We must dwell with Him every day. When we spend time in prayer and worship unto Him, we will find rest for our souls.

I love the Father. In His loving kindness and gentle way, He reminded His prophetess, His handmaiden, His daughter to "see" Him. He reminded me to focus on His abilities, His power, and His authority. My focus was no longer on the growth in my daughter's throat, but on the truth that by His stripes she is healed. And healed she was!

That word encouraged my heart, increased my faith, and gave me a blessed hope. This is one of the keys to victorious living. I pray that your spiritual eyes are opened and that you can see the unseen in your situation. I pray that the Spirit of the Lord causes you to see things, not according to the natural, but according to the spirit. I challenge you to open your eyes and see your situation from a different perspective. See it according to the word of God, His truth. Then dwell there and rest in Him.

My Autopilot Kicked In

"However, when He, the Spirit of truth, has come, He will guide you into all truth..." ~John 16:13 NKJV

I woke up refreshed and ready to go. My mind was focused, and I was pushing tasks quite early. However, just yesterday was a different story. Have you heard the saying "I'm so tired I can't see straight"? I had never experienced that personally until yesterday. I literally could not read what was in front of me. Focusing was so difficult to do. I knew I could read, but I had to rub my eyes multiple times just to get my eyes to focus on the words. Now, I know you're probably saying, "Girl, you just needed some glasses." (lol) That may be true, but yesterday was very different; I promise you.

I was so tired, and I think the only reason anything got done was because my "autopilot" kicked in (and God's grace, of course). It's days like that when I appreciate having a daily regimen and a to-do list. It's on days like yesterday, when my brain is functioning slow, that I appreciate the discipline the Holy Spirit developed in me over the years. Years ago, I decided, or should I say, agreed with God, to homeschool my children. The first year was a living H, E, double hockey sticks. I was overwhelmed and frustrated, feeling like I had made the biggest mistake of my life. I couldn't seem to get a grip on how to get *everything* done: school, cooking, training, teaching, cleaning, etc. Once again, I cried out to the Lord and once again, He answered.

It was not uncommon for my husband and I to attend two to three Christian conferences a year. We were young and hungry for the things of God. We would go to different conferences throughout the year looking for direction and encouragement. We have since settled down quite a bit, but the Lord encouraged our hearts and taught us many things during those years. One of the conferences we attended happened to be a prophetic conference. We spent a lot of time in the prophetic circles. At that conference, the Father answered my heart's cry and stirred a discipline in me that still resides with me today.

I recall the prophets saying to me during the time of personal ministry that the Holy Spirit was going to give me strategy for my household and that the Holy Spirit was going to show me how to organize my daily schedule so that I would have time for prayer, Bible study, practicing dance (I was in private lessons), preparing school lessons, and all of the many other chores that awaited a wife and mother of six children. Of course, tears just rolled down my eyes as they continued to speak over my husband and I because I knew these people had no idea that I had been crying out to the Lord for those very things.

The Lord was faithful to His word. Through months of hands-on training by the Holy Spirit, I was taught and given instruction on just how to organize my chaotic life. Those instructions from the Holy Spirit led to a peaceful, organized daily regimen, even giving me the freedom to strategize, instead of just functioning. There's a big difference. I had a choice. I could continue the way I was going in pure frustration or allow the Holy Spirit to disciple me. It was no easy task. My new-found strategy and organization required that I awake at 4:30 every morning. It meant that I had to follow the instructions of the Holy Spirit to the tee. A typical day consisted of early morning prayer and Bible study, dance practice, review of school lessons, fixing breakfast, bathing and dressing children, eating breakfast, two to three hours of school lessons, lunch, children's nap time (washed clothes during that time), afternoon snack, prep dinner, eat dinner and attend whatever church related events that were scheduled for the evening, evening snack, children's bedtime, mommy and daddy time, sleep, then awake to do it all over again.

At first, my mind, body and spirit fought this new schedule. I hated getting up early, believe it or not. Today, I wouldn't have it any other way! I decided to just yield and trust the Holy Spirit. After all the word says that He would lead us into all truth. It was all for my good. I am sharing this because those times of yielding to the Holy Spirit developed a discipline in me that is now my autopilot. The organization and strategy the Holy Spirit taught me developed times of discipline that kick in when I need them most. It's just like fire drills. You practice them when there's no fire, so that when there is a fire and you're panicky, your autopilot of discipline will kick in.

The same is true for our spiritual life. There are times when we are weary and tired, even overwhelmed by life and circumstances to the point where we can't see straight (spiritually). It's at those times that you can tap into your spiritual autopilot. The word of God that you have poured into your spirit, the relationship you've developed with the Lord, and the Holy Spirit all begin to arise in you on their own. It just pours out of you.

It's in those times when you appreciate the moments that you didn't feel like reading but did anyway. Or the times that you prayed even when you didn't feel like it. It's in those times that you're developing a discipline, doing your fire drills for those times of weariness and tiredness.

I'm amazed at the number of people who still don't take time to pray and study the word of God. I have heard every excuse from not having time to it's just boring. Yet, it's those same people who, in the time of trouble, don't have anything to tap into. They call me to call down the fire of God on their situation. Of course, I don't mind doing that. However, I believe that there should be a daily discipline of prayer and study (fasting too) in the life of every believer so that in times of trouble their autopilot will kick in. Then, instead of calling me in distress, they can call me to stand in agreement with the word of God that has already arisen in them. Amen.

I want to encourage you today to take time to pray and read the word of God every day. Create a discipline of feeding your spirit. You never know when life will hit or try to overwhelm you. It's in those times that our autopilot will kick in. It's those moments that the Holy Spirit will bring to your remembrance those scriptures you have been reading. It's in those times that strength arises in you because you know the God you serve because you've spent time in His presence. All that time David spent in the field tending the sheep and worshipping the Lord prepared Him for his position as king. Read the Psalms; whenever David struggled, whether it was with King Saul or other enemy kings, he always went back to that place of who God was. Remember, the Holy Spirit has to have something to bring to your remembrance.

I am so thankful for those years of pressing in to pray and study, even when I didn't want to. Those times were seeds to the fruit I see in my life today. When life seems overwhelming, scriptures that I may not have read in years will arise in my spirit and encourage my heart. That's my autopilot kicking in. I love it. If you're feeling tired, weary, or overwhelmed, let your autopilot guide you!

Choose to Rest & Rejoice In Jesus

"This is the day which the Lord hath made; we will rejoice and be glad in it." ~Psalms 118:24 KJV

Have you ever had one of those days where everything is going well until it isn't? I can vividly recall having one of those days with my eldest daughter. The day was going great and I felt like I was beating the clock. I was flowing through my to-do list in record time and I was pleased and thankful to the Lord at the accelerated progress. By the time the evening rolled around, I was able to do a few extra things like finish my homework as I was in school at the time. I was happy that I had a moment to relax. But as the saying goes, "All good things must come to an end." I don't necessarily buy into that phrase because it's not all true, but it seemed apropos for this story.

Against everything in me, I had agreed to allow my eldest daughter to borrow my car. Her outing was simple enough; she was headed to the store and dinner. The store was only two blocks away, and the restaurant was right next to it. I was still against letting her use the car, but my husband, who was helping me to "lighten up," convinced me to trust her. After all, it was only around the corner.

A couple hours passed, and I was sitting in my bed talking to a friend when I heard a grinding-type noise coming from outside out my bedroom window. I ignored it for about two to three minutes because I thought it was just my neighbors having some issues with their car. Finally, I got up and looked out the window. I saw my car, halfway up the drive, while the wheels turned and spun in place. It snowed that evening, but I thought, "It can't be that slippery." Quenton, our spiritually adopted son, went out to try to help push the car up the driveway. I quickly sent word to tell them to just stop. I was going to take care of my car myself.

I hurried and put on my shoes and coat, but by the time I got outside the car had been fully backed up the driveway. My daughter jumped out of the car and was headed into the house. I called to her to give me the keys because she had parked crooked and that would pose a problem later for my husband's car. As I approached the car, I noticed that it looked weird. It was leaning to one side. Then I saw it. The grinding noise I had heard earlier was the sound of my front left steel-belted radial tire and the rim being severely destroyed.

Words cannot express how angry I was. Well, they could, but I would never say those words here. (lol) I couldn't even talk to my daughter. I just went back into the house and went to my room. I called my husband several times. No answer. I knew he was in a rehearsal, but I didn't care. Finally, I shut down my computer and put away everything that I had been working on and just laid across my bed. I began to pray and ask the Holy Spirit to help me. I knew I needed to walk in forgiveness and mercy, but I was struggling for the moment. I knew my daughter hadn't destroyed my car on purpose, but I was quite angry with her. I knew she needed my mercy and forgiveness. I also knew that I had a full day ahead and I would need my car. "Help Lord," was all I could say. I didn't know how the Father was going to fix it, but I drifted off to sleep praying that He did. The Holy Spirit taught me how to rest in Him. He taught me to put things at the feet of Jesus and allow Him to be God.

When I woke up the next morning, I didn't know how the day would go as far as transportation and all. However, one thing that I rested in was that my heavenly Father had it all in His hands. I chose to rest in His promises that day. I kept His word before me (meditating); I was sure to cast down imaginations and to take into captivity every thought that exalts itself against the knowledge of God. (II Corinthians 10:5) I made a choice to trust in the Lord with all my heart and lean not to my own understanding. I chose to acknowledge Him in all my ways and trusted Him to direct my paths. (Proverbs 3:5-6)

This is the day that the Lord has made. Choose to rejoice and be glad in it!

Full Circle

The land, which we passed through to search it, is an exceeding good land. If the Lord delight in us, then he will bring us into this land, and give it us; a land which floweth with milk and honey. Only rebel not ye against the Lord, neither fear ye the people of the land; for they are bread for us: their defence is departed from them, and the LORD is with us: fear them not." ~Numbers 14:7-10 KJV

It had been some time since we had gotten together. Neither of us could seem to work it out in our schedule. Finally, we just locked down a day and didn't let anything get in our way. I was excited to finally sit down for dinner with one of my spiritual daughters, Sarah. I praised the Lord for the opportunity and His impeccable timing because our date was a divine appointment.

It was a delight to hear all that God was doing as she and I reminisced and caught up on what had been going on in each of our lives. We talked about everything from family to Obama and the health care bill. All of this was wonderful, but God had much in store for me. One of the things that was mentioned in our conversation became a catalyst to what the Holy Spirit wanted to speak to my heart, although I didn't know it at the time.

Sarah shared with me that she would be taking a trip out of the country to visit some of her friends and former students in a few weeks. She was very excited about the trip, especially since it had been at least a year since she had been there. This was the place that she had lived at a point in her life and wasn't sure when she would return. The Father was giving her the opportunity to go back. As she shared details of this trip, (when she was leaving, who she was visiting, where she was staying, and how long she would be there, and so on) the Holy Spirit began to speak to my heart. "Full Circle," is what I heard Him say.

Normally, I would have inquired more on that, but for some reason I didn't give much attention to it. Probably because I thought it was just Him giving a synopsis of where my spiritual daughter was in her life. He will often speak to me that way. He was, in fact, giving me a synopsis about Sarah, but I soon realized that He was also speaking concerning me and my life. Once I returned home, the Holy Spirit began to give me a download as I began to mentally recall my day and the recent conversation that I had with Sarah.

I was thinking about different parts of the wonderful fellowship and conversation that I had with my daughter. I smiled at some things, repented at others, and realized how much I cherished our relationship. When I began to recall the details of the trip that was planned, I heard the Holy Spirit say to me again, "Full Circle." I said to the Lord, "Okay, Father. I am listening." The Holy Spirit began to bring to my remembrance the significance of Sarah and I finally getting together for dinner and the significance of the trip she had planned.

You must understand that this was someone that I believe the Father brought us together. When I first met Sarah we instantly connected in the spirit. We both knew our newfound relationship was a God thing. This was confirmed through countless events and conversations as the years have gone by. As a matter of fact, the Lord had given me specific instructions on how Sarah and I were to relate to each other. The bond that He has given us is hard to explain. Often, the things going on in her life and in mine seem to parallel one another. It's not that we are doing the exact same thing, at the exact same time, all the time. But there are times when what God is doing in her life is almost identical to what He's doing in my life, whether it's building our faith, dealing with relationships, breaking old habits and thoughts, etc. Although there are different characters and plots, the principles are the same. It seemed that was a season where God was bringing our lives "full circle." All I could do was chuckle at God; He makes me laugh a lot!

Sarah and I were at a place in our lives where we were at the beginning of the point. It's as if, both spiritually and naturally, He was giving us a second chance to take another approach to the same promises that He spoke to us some time ago. I liken it to the children of Israel when they were released from the jaws of Egyptian slavery. God brought them out Egypt through the Red Sea and killed their enemies in the process. Yet, when they got to the doorway of the Promised Land, instead of believing that God was able to give them the land that He promised to them, they chose to murmur and complain. They allowed the "giants" in the land to keep them from taking what was rightfully theirs-- a land promised to them by God himself.

Now I'm not saying that Sarah and I were amongst those who were murmuring and complaining. My focus is on the fact that sometimes we suffer at the hands of the lack of faith and unbelief of our brothers and sisters. It's sad, but true. All suffered, including Joshua and Caleb, because of the unbelief, murmuring, and complaining of others. Despite the giants in the land, Joshua and Caleb still believed that God was able to give them their land. It was unfortunate that they had to suffer a forty-year journey along with all the non-believers and not enter the Promised Land until all had died.

This is the word the Lord was speaking to my heart. He was letting me know that He had brought me "full circle" back to the point of beginning. He was reassuring that the promises that He spoke to me many years ago were still yet mine. Although it seemed that I had been delayed, the Lord was making it clear to me that I would still see the promises and possess them. Hallelujah!

"For all the promises of God in him are yea, and in him Amen, unto the glory of God by us." ~(II Corinthians 1:20 KJV

Be encouraged, people of God. You may be waiting for the manifestation of a promise that God has spoken to you. It has been a frustrating time and season in your life. You have not understood the delay in seeing things coming forth. For some, the delay has not been your fault. The delay could be because of the unbelief, murmuring and complaining spirits of others. I believe that businesses, ministries, and other God ideas are held up because of those who won't sow money that I know the Lord has told them to (out of disbelief), those who speak negatively about everything and everybody (murmuring), and those who spend every waking hour working against instead of with those around them (complaining).

Now, I'm not telling you to start pointing fingers. God forbid. We have a real enemy with a daily goal to kill, steal, and destroy the followers of Jesus Christ. Whether the delay has been because of a person or otherwise, the culprit behind it all is satan, the evil one. Don't be fooled and begin to focus on the wiles of the devil, but rather keep your eyes on Him.

I believe that this is a season of coming "Full Circle." I believe that those who have put their trust in the Lord will walk in the promises that He has set before them. I believe that the forty-day season of killing off old thinking, old behaviors, and old relationships are coming to an end and that the Father is bringing those who have trusted, the Calebs and Joshuas, into their Promised Land.

I'm thankful to the Lord today that He sees my heart. I'm thankful for the "forty-year" journey and all that was broken off because of it. I'm thankful that despite the disbelief and mishandling of faith of others that I am not negated from His promises. I'm thankful that although there was a delay that I will yet walk into the Promised Land. Hallelujah!

"If ye be willing and obedient, ye shall eat the good of the land."
~Isaiah 1:19 KJV

Yet Will I Praise Him

"Even though the fig trees have no blossoms, and there are no grapes on the vines; even though the olive crop fails, and the fields lie empty and barren; even though the flocks die in the fields, and the cattle barns are empty, Yet I will rejoice in the Lord! I will be joyful in the God of my salvation!" ~Habakkuk 3:17-18 NLT

While my daughter completed school and worked, I agreed to watch my eldest grandchild, Danyal. His mom was a full student and a hairstylist, a combination that left her with little time to do anything else. Danyal spent most of his days with me, sometimes being with me ten to twelve hours a day. This was a challenge some days to my flesh, my spirit, and my mind. Children have a special way of working your nerves at times. During the time that I was caring for Danyal, my youngest child was fifteen, so the constant care of baby days were long gone for me. Yet, there I was starting all over with my almost two-year-old grandson, Danyal.

My daughter and I would often have had the discussion of public day care, but that conversation always ended with me saying, "I will just keep him." As much as it was an inconvenience for me, I loved my grandson to life and I just couldn't see him being raised by anyone other than his family. Call it the homeschooler in me. I just believe we must be diligent in, not just teaching academics to our children, but imparting the Word of God into their spirits. That impartation can only take place when we spend time with our children speaking, teaching, and praying over them. (Deuteronomy 11:18-19)

I mentioned my grandson because his actions became a catalyst to my deliverance from "stinkin-thinkin." One night, I had been sitting at my computer finishing up some travel arrangements and some dance related paperwork. Everyone had gone to bed, including my Danyal.

When I finished with the few things I was working on, I prepared to go upstairs to bed. My usual routine is to tidy up books and papers around me, turn out lights, lock the doors, and make sure dinner is put away. You know, shutting down the house kind of stuff. I turned around to look at my living room to kind of survey the land, and all I could do was shake my head in disgust.

My wonderful grandson had thrown his stuff all over the living room floor. There were toys, clothes, pillows, blankets, and more toys everywhere. The room had been cleaned and re-organized at least three times that day so I had a fit that it was out of order once again. I can be a neat freak at times and my grandson helped to break that spirit in me by default. Danyal seemed to see life differently. He was not a lover of order. He did his best every day to undo my acts of tidiness. I know you parents can relate!

Anyway, when I got upstairs to my room, I jokingly said to my husband, "Danyal makes my life a vicious cycle." We both laughed. As I was changing clothes for bed, I thought about the statement I had just made, and the Holy Spirit chimed in and began to speak to my heart. He began to show me that those words that I spoke were how I had been feeling the last few days. He was right, of course.

I had been in a spiritual battle in my mind. The enemy was riding me hard with thoughts of defeat and hopelessness. I was feeling like my life was a vicious cycle of doing the same thing repeatedly with no sense of true progression and change. I felt like every time I seemed to get some things together that the enemy came to wreak havoc and bring chaos once again. I felt like I was constantly giving, pouring, and giving more with seemingly little or no return. I was tired and weary in my spirit. I was tired of the war, tired of waiting, tired of wondering how my needs and desires would be met, and tired of standing. Of course, those were all feelings, not the truth.

When the Holy Spirit began to speak to me, I repented for allowing my feelings to get out of hand. I immediately took authority over that series of thoughts, casting them down in obedience to the word of God. (2 Corinthians 10:4-5) I began to thank the Lord for His faithfulness to me and began to declare the promises of God once again. I want to encourage you to do the same today.

Take a warfare stance in the spirit with me. Keep the Word of God before you, meditating on it day and night. (Psalm 1:1-3) Take courage in His faithfulness. Remember, we are in a war and the battleground is the mind. I believe that there will be great increase and growth, both naturally and spiritually, for the body of Christ. There will be open doors and great opportunities to share the gospel of Jesus. But I also believe that the enemies of God and warfare will increase, being very intense at times. I am reminded of the scripture in Lamentations, where it says, "...the enemy has enlarged himself." There is a war but know this--we are guaranteed to win. Hallelujah!

    I pray that you are victorious in your battle over ungodly thoughts today. I pray that as you meditate on the word that you will be encouraged to stand!

Be Persistent in Faith

"However, when the Son of Man comes, will He find [persistence in] faith on the earth?" ~Luke 18:8b AMPC

My grandson, Danyal, used to have a habit of grabbing my arm or hand and escorting me to whatever it is that he wanted. Although he was able to say a few words, most of the time his words were accompanied by a tugging or pulling action. One day, I was trying to get some work done and in came Danyal. He called my name and started pulling on my arm to go and get something from under the couch. Yanking my arm back, I told him that I would come and look in a minute. Well, Danyal was not having it. He kept grabbing my arms and saying, "Grandma, my car-truck!" As much as I tried to ignore him I couldn't. His persistent pulling, grabbing, and talking made me want to strangle him. (lol) Of course, I didn't, but I did finally stop what I was doing and get up to go to the couch.

    I knelt and looked under the couch and did not see anything. I looked up at him and said, "Danyal, there's no car-trucks under the couch." I then got up and went back to what I was doing. Well, Danyal fell out crying (which I ignored) and eventually came back over to me and began to pull and grab my arm again. With tears streaming down his face, he said to me, "Grandma, my car-truck!" while pointing to the couch. I bantered back and forth with Danyal for a short time trying to convince him that there was nothing under the couch. Again, he wasn't having it.

    Eventually, I gave in to his persistent pulling, grabbing, and talking and went back to the couch. Again, I knelt next to the couch, looked under it, and didn't see anything. I straightened up, looked Danyal in the eye and said, "Danyal, there's nothing under the couch." He looked back at me, as if my words had no meaning, and said, "Grandma, my car-truck!" and pointed at the couch.

Reluctantly I looked under the couch again, but that time I looked more closely. And lo and behold, all the way at the back end of the couch I could see a glimpse of some teeny tiny wheels. Danyal was right. His car-truck was under the couch. I grabbed a wooden spoon and slid it under the couch until the car-truck was visible. I grabbed it and gave it to him and boy, was he a happy camper. He went on to play with his car-truck and I went on to finish my business in peace!

I had to laugh when it was all said and done. I chuckled to myself as I thought, "This boy is persistent!" He wasn't going to give up until I got his car-truck from under the couch." I began to laugh out loud because I knew at that moment that the Lord was using Danyal to speak to my heart. Our Father knows us better than we know ourselves. And He knew that there were some things taking place in my attitude and spirit that He needed to deal with quickly.

My husband and I had recently received some not-so-good news and the issue seemed totally out of our control. That issue was heavy on my heart, even amid all the birthday preparation and celebrations and fulfilling dance responsibilities. I was not speaking of them much, but they were in my spirit. To deal with the stress of it all, at some point I subconsciously began to take on the *Que Sera Sera* attitude—"whatever will be, will be."

Now, if you don't know me well, I think "whatever" is from hell. It's not a stance, it's a cop out. And if you're copping out then you are not standing in faith (at least that's how I feel about it). Many of us hide behind "whatever" because we'd rather not take a stand than to take one and risk being disappointed. When we say, "whatever," we're saying, we don't trust that God will come through for us. Think about that. How insulting is it to say to the God of the universe "whatever"?
When that reality hit me, my heart and lips repented to the Lord because I was heading down that road of faithlessness. Thank God for the Holy Spirit and His love for us.

The persistence of Danyal was the Holy Spirit's way of reminding me to continue to press into prayer for the things that were concerning my heart. He was reminding me not to become complacent in my thoughts and prayers, embracing the Que Sera Sera attitude, but rather to be diligent and persistent in prayer to the Father, trusting that He loves me and that He will answer me in due season. The Holy Spirit led me to read the parable of the persistent widower. (Luke 18:1-8) In this parable, the widower had suffered an injustice by someone, and she relentlessly pleaded with the judge, day after day, to do something about it. This judge, whom the word of God says, neither feared God nor man, didn't readily respond to her. And why would he? He had no respect for God or man. Yet, because of this widow's persistence, this ornery, obstinate judge felt that he must respond, if only for the purpose of getting her to leave him alone.

"Then the Lord said, Listen to what the unjust judge says! And will not [our just] God defend and protect and avenge His elect (His chosen ones), who cry to Him day and night? Will He defer them and delay help on their behalf? I tell you, He will defend and protect and avenge them speedily." ~Luke 18:6-8 AMPC

    Jesus shares this parable with His disciples to show them that persistence pays off. He encouraged the disciples to continually ask the Father for what their needs and desires. Jesus specifically points out that this was a heathen, ungodly judge whose regard for anyone else, let alone God, was non- existent. Yet, he responded to the persistence of the widower. How much more would His Father, our Father, respond to us?
    That was surely an on-time word for me. Some of the situations and issues that my husband and I were facing were the result of an injustice. At that time, we had been praying about it for almost eight months. We certainly had moments of victory, but also countless moments of disappointments. My heart was so heavy over the matters that I was finding myself transitioning from the "our God is able" to the "whatever" attitude that I spoke of earlier. I found myself saying, "I'm just trusting God," but was I really trusting? No! I was copping out, if only just for a moment.
    Praise God for the Holy Spirit who brings us into all truth. The truth was that I was slowly letting go of my faith because I didn't want to be disappointed again. This is not the way a child of the King should live. Danyal bugging me was the Father's way of reminding me to take my stance in the spirit as I know to do. Reminding me to be the battle axe He's called me to be. Reminding me to be diligent, tenacious, and persistent in prayer before Him concerning the issue. He was letting me

know that He would respond. ***"...though He bears long with them...I tell you that He will avenge them speedily..." (Luke 18:7-8)*** Hallelujah!

I don't know what you're dealing with in your life right now. You may be facing marriage issues, financial issues, family issues, or other pressing things. I'm praying that you will grab ahold to this word today. Continue to be persistent in your prayers toward Him. He does hear you and He will respond. I pray that you will take a stand in the spirit today against the injustices that the enemy has sent your way. Know that Father God is your avenger and that you are His, the elect, and He will answer.

Father, I pray for Your people today. I pray that You would give us the courage to stand amidst injustice. Father, I pray that You will give us a heart to pray consistently and persistently toward You. I pray that You will continue to strengthen our faith and that we will learn more each day to trust You. Father, remind us, through the little things, that You have not forgotten us. Remind us to be as my grandson, Danyal, to keep at it until we see Your hand move. I love You today, Lord! In Jesus' name, Amen.

Hidden in the Cleft of the Rock

"And it shall come to pass, while my glory passeth by, that I will put thee in a clift of the rock, and will cover thee with my hand while I pass by: And I will take away mine hand, and thou shalt see my back parts: but my face shall not be seen." ~Exodus 33:22-23 KJV

Journaling is an outlet for me where I spend time sharing with Lord on the pages. I was thumbing through my journal and came across an entry that spoke to me. I don't often share from my journal, probably because many of the entries are very personal and intimate and speak directly to me. However, every once and a while I will share something that I feel may be a blessing to someone else or if I feel the Lord leading me to do so. The following was one of my shorter entries (mainly scripture verses), but I pray as you read the words that you will sense the gentle touch of the Holy Spirit. I know it brought encouragement and comfort to my heart and I pray that it will stir your heart toward Him as well. May you find peace and rest in His word today. Amen.

In early January 2009, the Holy Spirit led me to read Exodus 33. As I read it, I thought to myself, "Lord, where are you going with this?" I soon found out. In this passage of scripture, Moses spoke to God about leading His people on to the Promised Land. In the midst of getting instructions, Moses asked the Lord to see His glory. This was not Moses' first encounter with God; Moses had a close relationship with Father God. (Read through Exodus to see how their relationship developed.) He was aware of God's power, holiness, and sovereignty. Yet, Moses wanted to know God even more deeply. He wanted to see His glory.

"And the LORD said unto Moses, I will do this thing also that thou hast spoken: for thou hast found grace in my sight, and I know thee by name. And he said, I beseech thee, shew me thy glory. And he said, I will make all my goodness pass before thee, and I will proclaim the name of the LORD before thee; and will be gracious to whom I will be gracious, and will shew mercy on whom I will shew mercy. And he said, Thou canst not see my face: for there shall no man see me, and live. And the LORD said, Behold, there is a place by me, and thou shalt stand upon a rock: And it shall come to pass, while my glory passeth by, that I will put thee in a clift of the rock, and will cover thee with my hand while I pass by: And I will take away mine hand, and thou shalt see my back parts: but my face shall not be seen." ~Exodus 33:17-23 KJV

After reading this passage the Spirit of the Lord said to me, "Provision is in the cleft of The Rock!" And just as He hid Moses in the cleft as means of protection, provision and as a way for him to view and experience His glory, He was doing the same for me. The Father was reassuring me that He had made provision for me in the cleft of The Rock, Jesus Christ. Praise God! Everything that I needed was and is in Him (Jesus). His mercy is extended toward me in Jesus. His grace is extended toward me in Jesus. His love is extended toward me in Jesus. I get to experience, view, take in, encounter, and bask in His glory in Jesus. The Rock. What an awesome God we serve!

You must understand how great of a gesture this was from the Father toward Moses. No man (in human form) could see the Father and live. (Ex 33:20) However, the Father, out His love for Moses, found a way to allow Moses to see a glimpse of His glory. He hid him in the cleft of the rock. How awesome of a God that would go through the trouble of showing him (us) His glory. This was only a glimpse of the provision He had in store for us through the shed blood of His son, Jesus Christ. My spirit began to rejoice as I realized that the same was true for you and me this day. The Father, who loves us beyond words, was doing whatever was necessary for me to experience His glory and provision. *SELAH.*

Please understand that this word came at a time when life seemed to be overwhelming me. There was so much that was happening, and seemingly not happening, in my life at that time. The enemy was working hard to discourage me. satan was inundating me with thoughts of abandonment and failure. He was working hard to convince me that the Father had forgotten and abandoned me. Now, of course, I knew that wasn't true, but I tell you what, it sure did *feel* like it. If you're honest with yourself, you feel that way too at times.

Praise God for the Spirit of the Lord that lives in us, that leads us into all truth. And the truth is that He will never leave us nor forsake us. The truth is that He loves His children. The truth is that God is in control and there is nothing that is happening (or not happening) in our life that He doesn't know about. It's in those times that we must tap into the Spirit of God. We must rely on Him and not our emotions. We should never allow our emotions (soulish realm) to dictate our actions and responses. The enemy will trip us up every time.

I am so thankful today for the word of God. I'm thankful that my Father loves me. I'm thankful for the Holy Spirit that lives in me. I'm thankful that I am hidden in the cleft of THE ROCK, JESUS CHRIST. Hallelujah!

Dry Clean Only

"For my thoughts are not your thoughts, and neither are your ways my ways, saith the Lord." ~Isaiah 55:8 KJV

"DRY CLEAN ONLY"

That's what the label read. Yet, I decided, even reasoned with myself, that it would be alright. "It's cold water," I told myself. "It'll be just fine." I looked at the label again as I pulled my blouse out of the washing machine, shrunk to the size 2T! I wanted to cry. I did cry. Not because one of my favorite blouses was ruined, but because the Holy Spirit began to teach me a lesson. Stop trying to do things my way and trust the process that God has chosen for my life!

I must admit I've had this lesson before, but it seemed to really hit home as I stood in my laundry room at 5:00 am. There I was, holding a shriveled-up blouse in my hand. A blouse that was once beautiful to behold and the object of many compliments. I pulled and tugged at it, trying to stretch it to no avail. It was going to be that size forever. The more I pulled, the more I realized how big of a mistake I had made. I wanted to take it back, but I couldn't. The damage was done. The guilt of my foolish impatience began to eat at me. I walked up to my kitchen and the gentle teaching of the Holy Spirit was fast at work.

My mind was flooded with the thoughts and events of the last evening. I had gotten into a small disagreement with my daughter. I was frustrated, upset and ready for her to make some changes in her life. In a lack of wisdom, I tried to "help" her make some changes right then, right now. Again, I decided, even reasoned with myself, that I was right to "help." *Besides, I love her, and I have her best interest at heart. She needs to change NOW and appreciate it later.* Or so I thought. Of course, I felt my decisions would be best for her life. The whole thing ended badly.

The Holy Spirit helped me to see that I was treating my daughter just like I had treated my favorite top. I was trying to quicken change by changing the process. I was trying to make her "dry clean only" life fit into my wash and wear schedule. I was trying to do things my way and not trusting God's ways or His process. I wanted my daughter clean and ready to go ASAP. However, the cost is great when we try to adjust God's process without His leading. The situation ended with hurt feelings, pain, and despair. Oh, how I wept and repented to the Lord when I got the revelation. I immediately asked the heavenly Father for forgiveness. I had tried to change His process without His consent and made a huge mistake.

Thank God for His mercy and grace. I praise Jesus that the prompting of the precious Holy Spirit caught me early in my quest for change long before I could cause irreparable damage. I realized that it is critical that I entrust my daughter wholly to the Lord Jesus Christ and His process for her life. It is critical that I trust that God the Father knows how to make her life beautiful and knows how to make her the object of many compliments. Or she, like my blouse, could end up shrunken and unusable. Of course, the enemy would love that.

Are you trying to change God's process? Are you submitting to the process He's chosen for your life? Have you become impatient, frustrated, tired and ready for a quick change? I want to encourage you to keep putting your trust in the Father. No matter how bleak a situation may look, remember God is in control. We must learn to yield ourselves to God's ways. He has a specific process for your specific situation and His results are life-giving and eternal. Hallelujah!

Maybe you have already put the "dry clean only" in the wash, and damage may have come as a result. Damage to your heart, your finances, your children, and your marriage may be your experience. Know that God is a restorer. Unlike my blouse, our hearts and lives can be repaired and restored. The heavenly Father knows how to bring all things back to their original state. That's what salvation is all about--being restored to a relationship with the heavenly Father through the shed blood of Jesus. All you and I need to do is repent and submit to His process. The word of God says, **"If my people, which are called by my name, shall humble themselves, and pray, and seek my face, and turn from their wicked ways: then will I hear from heaven, and will forgive their sin, and will heal their land." (2 Chronicles 7:14)**

Burning Both Candles at the End with a Stick

"And the prayer of faith shall save the sick, and the Lord shall raise him up; and if he have committed sins, they shall be forgiven him. Confess your faults one to another, and pray one for another, that ye may be healed. The effectual fervent prayer of a righteous man availeth much." ~James 5:16-17KJV

Several years ago, I was privileged to be a part of a ministry launching in Paducah, Kentucky. A very dear friend of mine was kicking off her first gathering for her women's ministry called Willow Tree. I was on program to dance and to speak prophetically over the ministry. The spiritual warfare was quite intense, but the Lord was with me through it all; I was victorious!

It was a great time, but the wear and tear to my body was unreal. I'm usually pushing long days, up early and to bed late. That would be no big deal back in the day in my young twenties. However, I am not twenty anymore and my body and mind (can't say my spirit because it's always up), has its own time to completely shut down. Anyone who has ever roomed with me knows that to be true. (lol) If I sit or lay down after a long day, it's over. You can talk and I may be listening and might even respond, but I can't promise you that what comes out of my mouth will make any sense whatsoever.

One of the nights that we were in Paducah, my girlfriend came into the room where I was staying and sat on the couch across from me talking and sharing. I was trying to listen intently, but I could feel my brain shutting down. I was trying hard not to fall asleep, but the next thing I knew I awakened to my name being called. We both laughed and my girlfriend said, "You need to go on to bed." I replied, "Yeah, I do, and you do too." Then I said, as if to reprimand her, "You can't be burning both candles at the end with a stick!" Of course, she looked at me and we both laughed again. I said, "You know what I mean."

The next day my girlfriend told me that she couldn't go to sleep from laughing at what I said. She has a contagious type of laugh; once she starts, it's hard for her to stop. She ended up being awake another twenty to thirty minutes laughing. When she told me about it the next day we laughed again, reiterating the fact that I lack the ability to be cognizant when I'm sleepy.

About a week after that, I woke up and could hear myself saying, "...burning both candles at the end with a stick." I was still half asleep and had to really control myself to keep from busting out laughing. My husband would have surely confirmed his suspicions that his wife is a tad bit crazy! For some reason, I couldn't seem to shake the thought and could feel myself losing control, so I quietly got out of the bed to let my laugh out. (And let me say this--our heavenly Father has a wonderful sense of humor.) After I calmed down a bit, I said to the Lord, "What's that all about?!" I just knew that it was not coincidental that I awoke thinking about that, and I was right. The Holy Spirit was waiting patiently to speak to my heart.

Life can be so busy at times, and it can feel like you are burning candles at both ends. It's full of demands, most of which are not really that important when compared to the larger scheme of things. I'm learning that we often stress ourselves over things that we usually can't change and if we are honest, those things are usually linked to one of three things: the lust of the flesh, the lust of the eyes and the pride of life. (I John 2:16) Yet, mixed in the middle of all of that are a few things that are for the kingdom and our heavenly Father. I have been challenged by the Holy Spirit more than once to evaluate and reevaluate the things that are important. I am frequently faced with having to make a choice between doing what the Holy Spirit desires and what I feel that I need to cross off my to-do list. Of course, He wins every time and I love that.

We must remember to be sensitive to the Holy Spirit during our candle burning. Many times, I have changed and adjusted my schedule to make time to pray for family and friends about financial, physical, and family issues. There are many, including myself, who face tremendous and difficult situations that require the hand of God to move quickly. The Holy Spirit reminds me that taking a minute to pray might just be the answer to someone's breakthrough. For that reason, I endeavor to pray on their behalf, believing the Father for breakthrough every time. This is, or should be, the template life for all Spirit-led believers. After all, our life is not our own and because of who we are and whose we are, we are sometimes positioned, shifted, and adjusted in our everyday schedule to meet the needs of others, even when we may have needs ourselves. It's in those times that you can trust that the Father is taking care of all that concerns you, while you're taking care of all that concerns Him--His people.

    I don't advocate for burning your candle at both ends, but sometimes we just end up there. I understand that. I need and ask the Holy Spirit to help me with having healthy boundaries. However, I am praying that if you and I are burning both candles at the end with a stick, that it's for His glory and not our own. Praying that you experience His love today. Praying that you allow for divine interruptions and that you allow the Holy Spirit to work through you!

It's Just My Angel

"For it is written, He shall give his angels charge over thee, to keep thee." ~Luke 4:10 KJV

I used to get speeding tickets all the time when I lived in Detroit years ago. I lived in the city, near the new center area and I used to travel two to three times a week to Troy, Michigan for dance lessons. I would take I-75 by storm, driving from E. Grand Blvd in Detroit to Crooks Road in Troy, all in about twenty minutes. For those of you who are not from Detroit, this meant I was driving way over the speed limit. In hindsight, I am so grateful for the loving protection and faithfulness of the Lord. I was reckless and foolish, and I know there were angels watching over me. I am so thankful that Father God doesn't reward us according to our iniquities (Psalm 103), but He extends His grace and love toward us, even when we're on the nut.

I don't know if it was my young age, lack of skill, or both, but I was always getting pulled over by the police. I think I went to court at least four times for those darn tickets. Each time I received one, I would repent bitterly to the Lord. After all, I knew I was wrong. I would then plead to the Lord to extend grace and mercy toward me, crying for favor with the judge and the officers. Fortunately for me, the Father was always "faithful and just to forgive."

Every time I went to court, the judge would extend mercy toward me mainly because I had a good driving record. Go figure! The judge would not allow the ticket to be put on my permanent record and would fine me whatever the law allowed. That kept the infraction from being reported to my insurance company causing my premium to increase. Each time I would leave the courthouse thankful and humbled by the Father's grace.

Now you would have thought that each courthouse scare would get me, right? Oh, nooo! I would go out and do it all over again. It wasn't necessarily intentional, but I somehow found myself in the same predicament. I remember the last time I got a ticket. I was, once again, heading back home from dance lessons in Troy. Although that time I only repented; I didn't ask God for mercy. I was going to take my punishment. I knew better and I thought that I should suffer the consequences of my actions. Praise God that He doesn't listen to our stupid logic. The Father decided to extend what I call extreme mercy toward the one ticket that I desired to be punished for. The extent of the favor and grace that the Father gave concerning that ticket broke something in my spirit in a good way.

It was a wonderful testimony of God's unconditional love. Basically, the state trooper who issued the ticket showed up to court on his day off and argued my case in my favor. He found a clause in the law about having a good driving record, which I knew wasn't true, but my record showed me being clean. By the way, that's how the blood of Jesus cleanses us. It washes our slates clean, every day. The Father only sees the purity of His son for those who are under the blood of Jesus. It doesn't matter what we've done in the past, all have been washed clean. Hallelujah! The state trooper exchanged a bunch of legal jargon with the judge and somehow was able to get the ticket that he issued dismissed altogether.

I stood in that courtroom amazed and humbled at God's faithfulness and love for me. It made me want to get it together. I never wanted to end up in court again for speeding tickets, and I haven't since that day. The Word of God is true when it says, *"...the goodness of God leadeth thee to repentance..." (Romans 2:3)*

I repented to the Lord for my lack of self-control (which is a fruit of the spirit) and for my disobedience to Him. I really wanted to change and cried out to the Lord to help in that area. Of course, the Lord answered. In addition to listening and responding to the Holy Spirit and being more aware of my surroundings, the Lord sent angels to watch over me. Angels that would bring me into remembrance of the Fruit of the Spirit: love, joy, peace, longsuffering, gentleness, goodness, faith, meekness, and temperance (self-control). (Galatians 5:22-23)

I would be driving down the road and an angel would pull in front me and drive 50 mph for twenty miles. I would have a fit, fussing and trying to figure out how to get around them, but to no avail. It was a set-up, of course. This happened repeatedly for several weeks, until one day I realized that it was the Father's way of looking out for me. From then on, instead of getting upset I began to thank the Lord for loving me so much to send His angels to keep me on track. To this day, whenever someone gets in front of me that makes me slow down, I say to myself, "It's just my angel."

Over the years, I have come to appreciate my angels and I began to recognize them, not just when I was driving. I recognized them when I was standing in line at the store, or trying to get that special parking spot, or even when I am waiting in the drive-thru line at the bank. The Lord would send angels to get in front of me or to wait on me that were challenging to my flesh. These angels were sent to help me with patience, kindness, longsuffering, and temperance. I have come to know that there are angels all around sent to not only protect, but to help you and me grow.

We serve a loving God who is willing to do whatever it takes to help us walk worthy of our calling in Christ Jesus. So, the next time you're being challenged to slow down, be patient, operate in self-control, or extend some mercy, know that you're probably dealing with an angel sent to sharpen you and keep you on track.

Breaking Forth

"Then shall thy light break forth as the morning, and thine health shall spring forth speedily: and thy righteousness shall go before thee; the glory of the Lord shall be thy reward." ~Isaiah 58:8 KJV

Busy. I hate that word, but it seems to be the best word to describe my life when my daily to-do list seems to get longer and longer. It seems the more that I get done the more there is to be done. I am sure someone can relate to that. I hate being busy, believe it or not. Many times, the schedule that I live is not my schedule of choice. It's simply what must be done for my family, my business, and for ministry. If there's purpose behind it and I know that it's going to bless and build others, I am more than willing to do it. Yes, it can be very tiring to the body and spirit, but in the end it's worth it.

During that kind of busyness, it's always a blessing when the Father shines on you. During a beautiful week in Chicago, I felt He did just that. The sun was shining through my window every morning and put a huge smile on my face. I think it was the sense of hope because it was a sign that spring was nearing. I could hear the scripture in **Habakkuk 2:3** ringing in my heart: **"For the vision is yet for an appointed time, but at the end it shall speak, and not lie: though it tarry, wait for it; because it will surely come, it will not tarry."** I was waiting with great anticipation.

Life can be busy and sometimes that busyness becomes a cloak of heaviness that you just want to cast off. Add to that the dreariness of the winter months and life just seems heavy. When I saw the sunshine and the consistent beautiful weather, my soul rejoiced. I don't know about you but, I need that sunshine. I need those rays of hope.

As I gazed out the window, I began to thank the Lord for the sunshine and for seasons. I began to tell Him that although I understood the need for winter that I was extremely delighted that the seasons were changing. I shared with Him how I just wanted to shed the heaviness that came with the winter season, both spiritually and naturally. I expressed my desire to be loose and free, letting down my hair. As I continued to commune and worship with Him, the Lord said to me "Daughter, you will break forth like the morning." As the words were being spoken, I could literally see in a vision the manifestation of the words coming alive. The vision was beautiful, arrayed with color and splendor--too much to try to describe here.

I began to weep, letting the comfort of His voice and words resonate in my heart. To be honest, I really don't know how to put into words how my spirit feels at moments such as those. You see, I know the Father sees all of me and knows the deep thoughts of my heart. When He speaks to me, those words are never surface. Many times, He is speaking to deep things in me that no one knows of. I struggle even now to articulate what all was addressed in that one phrase. Just know that the Father loves you and me. That love runs deep. And when you love Him in return you begin to hear His heartbeat in the deep. The word is true, "deep calls unto deep." (Psalm 42:7)

"Then shall thy light break forth as the morning, and thine health shall spring forth speedily: and thy righteousness shall go before thee; the glory of the LORD shall be thy reward." ~Isaiah 58:8 KJV

I have read this passage in the past, but of course, the Holy Spirit was giving more insight and revelation as I read it again. This promise of breaking forth is likened unto the promise of spring. It is a word of hope that He is going to do what He promised. It's a reminder that His word will be fulfilled in its season. Just as the seasons change and shift and have for over two thousand years, the same will be true in our lives. A new season will take place. It's a reminder of the Lord's faithfulness and that He has not forgotten His promises. It's a reminder that His word is yet alive and accomplishing all that He has set it forth to accomplish in the earth. (Isaiah 55:10-11) It's a reminder that every season has an end and a new one must begin. It's a reminder the Father God is not slack concerning His word: ***"He who begun a good work in you will be faithful to complete it." (Philippians 1:6)***

I believe that this is a word not only for me, but for many that have been experiencing a season of heaviness, coupled with a winter season (trying times). I believe that the Breaking Forth is here, even upon us. The Father is bringing us into a place that we can cast off the weights of the last season allowing us to let down our hair, so to speak, and be loosed in the spirit.

I believe that this Breaking Forth brings with it a new hope. Hope for the unexpected; hope for the impossible; hope for the seemingly lost and unreachable. I believe that this Breaking Forth will cause many, including myself, to walk in new levels of faith, to try new things, and to dare to walk on the water. I believe that the timing of Breaking Forth is orchestrated by the Father allowing many to get to such a place of desolation (dying to self) that a stirring takes place within us if we've yielded to the Spirit. So much so that when freedom comes our whole mindset will be different. No longer will there be insecurities, inefficiencies, and inadequacies an excuse. This Breaking Forth will debut the new and accentuate the old. Many who are seasoned in Him will declare His name with power and accuracy and many that are not-so-seasoned will break the chains of the enemies with boldness and courage. Hallelujah!

I get excited about spring, but I am more excited about Breaking Forth. Praying that you embrace your new season.

Wind Beneath My Wings

Did you ever know that you're my hero?
You're everything I wish I could be.
I could fly higher than an eagle,
for you are the wind beneath my wings.
Did I ever tell you you're my hero?
You're everything, everything I wish I could be.
Oh, and I, I could fly higher than an eagle,
for you are the wind beneath my wings,
'cause you are the wind beneath my wings.
Oh, the wind beneath my wings.
You, you, you, you are the wind beneath my wings.
Fly, fly, fly away. You let me fly so high.
Oh, you, you, you, the wind beneath my wings.
Oh, you, you, you, the wind beneath my wings.
Fly, fly, fly high against the sky,
so high I almost touch the sky.
Thank you, thank you,
thank God for you, the wind beneath my wings.
(partial lyrics from Hero by Bette Midler)

When I was in Indianapolis, I didn't get much sleep. Between traveling late, getting up early, extremely long days and the Father waking me up to talk, sleep was not happening. It was all good, however. The Father was giving me some serious downloads while I was away, so the lack of sleep was worth it.

As I have mentioned before, the Father speaks to me quite often through visions, kind of like dreams, except that I am usually wide awake. One of the visions that He showed me that weekend in Indianapolis was of me standing on a cliff very high up on a mountain top. I was walking back and forth on the edge of the cliff, teeter-tottering every now and then, almost falling off into the open space below. I was at peace, even happy it seemed, feeling free as I played along the edge of the cliff. There was no fear; I didn't seem to be scared at all. As a matter of fact, it was as if I was waiting for the Lord to give the word that I could freely fall into the open space. I wanted Him to just tip me on over. I was ready…I am ready to fly.

I think the Holy Spirit was standing next to me waiting for me because as soon as I awoke, I heard Him begin to sing to me the lyrics from the song Hero. *"You (the Lord) are the wind beneath my wings. Fly, Fly away…"* is what I heard Him say. Hero is one of my favorite songs. Bette Midler can really sing the song so well. I cry every time I hear it. I think it has such a message of unselfishness and honor to those who inspire us. I have several people in my life that fit that description, but today I only want to speak about the One, who not only undergirds me with the wind of His spirit, but who gives me the wings necessary to fly.

When I heard the Holy Spirit singing over me, it took me back to that vision of being on the cliff. It was as if the Lord was showing me that I had been tipped over that cliff. I freely fell into the open space, and all I needed to do was spread my wings. It was as if the Lord was saying to me that it's time to fly and that He would be the wind beneath my wings. I can't even begin to tell you how I felt at that moment. Tears of joy were flowing at the faithfulness of the Father. It's hard to explain how big it was to me but know this--what the Lord showed me in the spirit with that vision coupled with what the Holy Spirit spoke to me in Indianapolis was a prophetic vision of what was to come.

Shortly after my out-of-town encounter with the Lord, I received confirmation that I would be a part of a major Christian dance production opportunity. The production required me to travel throughout the United States for training and then minister the production in other nations. It was an opportunity that I would have never dreamed of, especially at my age. Yet, I knew it was God's timing. The producer told me that he could see that "it was time for me to go to the nations." He went on to say that he could see that I was called to the nations but had been waiting and waiting. He was right. Years ago, the Lord had spoken many words over my life about me being called to the nations. At one point, I had just given up on that word thinking that I had misinterpreted it. I thought maybe it meant my offspring would go to the nations because all but one of them have been to foreign nations at least twice. However, I must admit within the year before my cliff vision, the

Holy Spirit had been stirring me once again with longing to go to the nations. I embraced the stirring, taking on the attitude of Mary--"Be it unto me Lord," not having any idea what the Father had planned.

Although my heart had been crying out for the past few years over promises that the Father spoke to my husband and I many years ago, I was still trusting that He knew what was best for us. You see, the Master Gardener, our Father, pruned us to the point that we almost looked desolate and unusable. Of course, that was not true, but it certainly seemed that way. Why all the pruning? The same reason every gardener prunes--to bear more fruit.

Oftentimes, I had questioned the Lord, not on His faithfulness to fulfill His promises, but when the pruning process would be over. *"When God, when"* is what I kept saying. At the same time, I knew deep down in my spirit that He had all things in His control and that He had great plans for Albert and me. I knew that He had not forgotten His promises concerning us. The news that I would be a part of the production was the beginning of the manifestation of some of those promises. Hallelujah!

When the Holy Spirit spoke to me about being the wind beneath my wings, I knew what that meant. It meant that the Lord had indeed tipped me over the edge. It meant that I was free falling into His promises (scary and exciting all at the same time). I won't pretend like I instantly knew what all of that would look like in the natural because I was flying in faith. What I do know is that He is the wind beneath my wings, and I heard Him say to me, "FLY!"

I just love the Lord. And each day, every morning it seems, I get a glimpse of how much He really loves me. I pray that you will know how much He loves You today. I pray that you will see and experience Him in the small things. I pray that you will know that His thoughts toward you are good to give you an expected end. (Jeremiah 29:11) And more than anything, I pray that He will be the wind beneath your wings today and always.

Country Girl

"Blessed shall you be in the city, and blessed shall you be in the country." ~ Deuteronomy 28:3 NKJV

I'm a city girl, born and raised. I grew up in cramped neighborhoods with houses that were probably only three feet apart. I could literally look out my kitchen window and see and talk to my neighbor without hollering. Everyone seemed to be right on top of each other. I didn't think anything of this until I started encountering friends who loved country living. Once, I visited my best friend in Kentucky. Whether she thinks so or not, she is a country girl to heart with a serious city-girl flare. As far back as I can remember, she has always wanted to have a house out in the middle of nowhere, where you must drive ten miles to see your neighbor. That is not my kind of living. However, this was the ideal life of those, including my friend, who liked living in the country.

I could appreciate the country living after returning home late one night from traveling for several days. Although I had a great time while I was away, my body and my spirit were weary, and I was longing to have a moment to spread out and relax before taking on the many tasks that were awaiting my return. Once I arrived at my boarding gate, I could quickly see that my desire to chill on the flight home was not going to happen. The flight was packed, not one seat was left open; there was no spreading out for me. I could feel the world closing in on me as I had no choice but to take a middle seat on the crowded flight home. I hate the middle seat! I could feel my shoulders swelling up as I tried to make myself comfortable, which never happened. The flight was late leaving and then delayed on the runway, until finally being released to take off. All those mishaps caused our flight to be about twenty minutes behind. By the time I arrived in Chicago I was so tense that I was about ready to smack somebody. Of course, I didn't, but I wanted to!

I could feel the weights of responsibility, one by one, taking their rightful place on my shoulders: wife, mom, ministry leader, business owner, Bible student, choreographer, financial deadlines, etc. I just wanted to scream. I began to reflect on my week and think of the beautiful countryside that I had seen. I stared out the window as my husband and I drove home, adding words to the conversation here and there, but longing to be out in one of the many country fields I had seen. I imagined running freely through the land. I knew then that I had to quickly reposition myself, get a hold of my thoughts, lest the enemy lead me down a wrong road. My heart began to cry out (silently) to the Lord to help me focus on Him and that place of rest and peace in Him.

"For he that is entered into his rest, he also hath ceased from his own works, as God did from his. Let us labour therefore to enter into that rest, lest any man fall after the same example of unbelief." ~Hebrews 4:10-11 KJV

Praise God for His faithfulness. His grace sustained me through the tasks of the evening, and I was able to sleep well, awakened in the morning refreshed and ready to face the day. As soon as I opened my eyes, the Holy Spirit began to speak to me about the countryside and I decided at that moment to become a spiritual country girl. I began to press into that spiritual countryside in Him -- the countryside that is never ending, the expansion of which there is no end. I found myself running with the Holy Spirit in the fields of the Spirit through worship. The fields that are full of joy and peace and liberty. As I spent time in His presence, I found myself repositioned. I found rest for my soul. Hallelujah!

"City" life can be overwhelming at times, but it's in those times that the Father reminds me that it never will be about my abilities. It's all about His. The same is true for you. When you find yourself being overwhelmed by the "city" life, purpose to reposition yourself. Press into His presence through worship and allow the Holy Spirit to guide you and show you how to cease from your works and enter that place of rest and peace in Him. Know that He has all things in His hands.

Today, walk in His grace, minute by minute, being empowered by the Holy Spirit. I pray that you find rest, peace, and liberty in Him.

His Covenant is Eternal

"God says, 'If my covenant with day and my covenant with night ever fell apart so that day and night became haphazard and you never knew which was coming and when, then and only then would my covenant with my servant David fall apart and his descendants no longer rule." ~Jeremiah 33:19-20 MSG

I woke up with a heavy heart. I found myself struggling with insecurities and inefficiencies in reaching the "mark" (Philippians 3:14). It was so heavy that I didn't want to even approach the Father in prayer. I felt like the prophet Isaiah when He said, **"Then said I, Woe is me! for I am undone; because I am a man of unclean lips, and I dwell in the midst of a people of unclean lips..." (Isaiah 6:5)** The Lord was not unaware of my feelings, nor is He unaware of yours. He knows that we all have moments such as this. After all, He is a Holy God.

However, we must be careful that we don't fall for the enemy in those times. His goal is to keep you from the presence of the Lord. Why? Because He knows that there is liberty in the presence of the Lord and that the Father's love will bring revelation and healing. **"Where the Spirit of the Lord is there is liberty." (II Corinthians 3:17)** So, as much as I wanted to hide myself in busy work and shy away from Him, I knew I needed to do just the opposite; I had to press into His presence.

I did what I do every morning. I got my Bible, my journal, a cup of coffee, and my worship music. As I began to sing and worship the Holy Spirit, that spirit of heaviness began to leave, and the Holy Spirit began to speak. It's good to be obedient. The Lord began to press on my heart a scripture that He had given me the day before: Jeremiah 33. I had been praying for my two best friends, both of which were in places in their lives where they were being catapulted into the promises of God. My girlfriend who lived in Arizona had just debuted her long-awaited album.

And my other girlfriend that lived in Kentucky was preparing for the grand opening of her second store and the launching of her distribution center. There were even things in the works for me. Although the Lord gave quite a few insights into what He was going to do in our lives, the part that rang in my spirit that morning was verses 19-22. They spoke of the covenant God made with David and how it could not be broken.

"God says, 'If my covenant with day and my covenant with night ever fell apart so that day and night became haphazard and you never knew which was coming and when, then and only then would my covenant with my servant David fall apart and his descendants no longer rule. The same goes for the Levitical priests who serve me. Just as you can't number the stars in the sky nor measure the sand on the seashore, neither will you be able to account for the descendants of David my servant and the Levites who serve me.'" ~Jeremiah 33:19-22 MSG

    The Lord began to remind me of His covenant with me. The Holy Spirit brought to my remembrance that His covenant is unbreakable. The only way that I could be separated from Him is if I chose to walk away. The word of God says that, **"...It is Christ that died...who also maketh intercession for us. Who shall separate us from the love of Christ? shall tribulation, or distress, or persecution, or famine, or nakedness, or peril, or sword? For I am persuaded, that neither death, nor life, nor angels, nor principalities, nor powers, nor things present, nor things to come, nor height, nor depth, nor any other creature, shall be able to separate us from the love of God, which is in Christ Jesus our Lord." (Romans 8: 34-39)**
    Think about that, there is NOTHING that can separate you from His love. This is His promise to you and me. And on top of that, Jesus himself intercedes on our behalf. He is our mediator: **"For there is one God, and one mediator between God and men, the man Christ Jesus." (I Timothy 2:5)** What an awesome God we serve!
    Even as I was meditating on the impenetrable covenant, the Holy Spirit reminded me of the story of the Prodigal Son in Luke 15. Here the young son chose to leave his father's house, to leave from under his covering and go at it alone. The scripture says he went and wasted all his inheritance until he was at a place of desolation and desperation. It

didn't help that there was also a famine in the land. It was not easy for him to find that which would replenish him and his way of living. He ended up with a job taking care of pigs. He was so desperate that, according to the Bible, he desired to eat the pig's feed. It's at that point that he "came to himself." (Luke 15:17) In other words, he got what I call a reality check. It's at that point that he realized that he chose to walk away from a good thing. His father's servants were living better than him. He realized how blessed he was to be in his father's house.

The same is true for us. There are times when we choose to turn away from the covenant that the Father put before us. We choose to walk away from Him through disobedience of His word and His counsel by the Holy Spirit. We choose to make stupid choices that only lead to desolation and desperation, with no way of replenishment; there is still a famine in the land. What a horrible place to be--hungry with no sense of relief. I am so thankful that the pig pen was not the end of this story.

The Bible says that the prodigal decided to go back home to his father. He chose to turn (repent) from his wasteful ways of living and return to his father's house. One would think that his homecoming would be anything but joyful. Yet, the Lord shows us a beautiful parallel of His covenant and unconditional love for us through the story of the prodigal. As his father waited with open arms, the prodigal returned home. The father even killed the fattened cow for him to celebrate his son's homecoming. It didn't matter where he had been, what he had done, or why he had chosen to come home. The father was only glad that his son had returned.

Isn't that just like our heavenly Father? When we get off track, whether small or big, the Father is always ready with open arms to forgive us and receive us back to Him. That's true covenant. That's true love. The Father never wavers in His love for us. It never dissipates. His blood covenant, through Jesus Christ, still covers us. No matter what. Even when we choose to walk away from Him, He never chooses to walk away from us. Hallelujah! I just love the Lord!

I pray that you press into His presence today. I pray that the Holy Spirit brings to your remembrance the covenant that you have with the Father. I pray that as you meditate on that covenant that you realize how much you are loved by Him. Whether you are dealing with marriage issues, family issues, or financial issues, know you can always run to your Father. He is always waiting with open arms to receive you, comfort you, and even celebrate over you.

He Danced with Me

"And their eyes were opened, and they knew him; and he vanished out of their sight. And they said one to another, Did not our heart burn within us, while he talked with us by the way, and while he opened to us the scriptures?" ~Luke 24:31-32 KJV

I was working on choreography for my dance classes and some ministry opportunities that were coming up. When I started into my two-hour practice, I was really struggling with ideas; I couldn't seem to get into the music. I know the struggle was partially because I had a very long day and there was entirely too much on my mind. Plus, I was in creative overload. I had been working on various projects the previous weeks and my mind was tired. Additionally, I had not had any down time to gather my thoughts, so my brain was still flooded with the cares of life. These things are a creative person's worst enemy.

I needed to do something to relax and release. I decided to start out with some worship music rather than jump right into choreography. I put on one of my old CDs from Cece Winans. It had been about three years since I had listened to that CD. I listened to the music and allowed my mind and body to be consumed with the rhythm and words. I began to dance and free flow, while incorporating some stretches to warm up my muscles. It felt good to my body and soul to be non-committal in my movement. Dancing free always feels good to me. Often, it's my escape from the cares of life. I could feel my body loosening up, but for some reason my mind was still struggling with thoughts from the day. Finally, after about three songs, I got a little breakthrough.

It was time to get on with the business of the day, which included choreographing three songs. I worked on the songs diligently, praying and asking the Holy Spirit to help the whole time. I knew that I wasn't in my usual creative flow and that I was going to have to trust what I knew from training and experience to get the job done. Although I worked on each song, I can't say that I accomplished what I would have wanted to in that time. I knew it was just not happening that day. If you're a creative, you know exactly what I mean. When it's there it's there, and when it's not, it's not.

I was quite disappointed with myself. I just couldn't get myself out of that funk, so I decided to work on one more piece before I called it quits for the night. It was a song that I was very familiar with, but I needed to get it done because I would be ministering to it that weekend. I wasn't looking to choreograph the piece, per se. I wanted to listen to it and get it into my spirit so that I could really minister the song. Whenever I'm given an opportunity to dance solo, I try not to choreograph it too tough. I prefer much more to free-flow. It's my opportunity to dance freely before the Lord; with teams, that is not always possible. When opportunities come when I can dance alone my heart rejoices.

I listened, danced, and prayed as the song played in the sound system. I began to dance to the music, singing the lyrics as I moved. At times I stopped to see where and how I wanted to flow with a particular section. I did that several times, playing the song repeatedly. About the third time through the song, suddenly, it felt like someone ran up behind me and hugged me, gently placing their hand on my shoulder. My heart began to race, and the tears began to flow. I knew it was Him. What I thought was me getting a flow was Him joining in my dance and worship. I was alone with Him and it was just us dancing. The song was my prayer and worship to Him.

His presence was beautiful, peaceful, and comforting in ways I cannot explain. I was overwhelmed with His gentleness and love, knowing that He could see my heart. The tears rolled down my face as I found myself enveloped in His presence. I danced harder and freer as long as my body would permit. It was my time with Him. I love when He surprises me and shows up unexpectedly in the midst of doing what I do. Even now as I think about how much He loves me, my eyes well up with tears.

Know that He loves you, too. When you're going through your day and it seems mundane, repetitious, and unrelenting, remember that the Father makes surprise visits. He will show up as you are continuing on your way and doing what you know to do, to refresh and restore you. It reminds me of one of my favorite Bible passages, the story of the Road to Emmaus found in Luke 24.

My prayer is that you will have that unexpected visit from the Lord in the days to come...maybe even today!

Ascending with Him

"The heavens declare the glory of God; and the firmament shows His handiwork." ~Psalm 19:1 NKJV

I absolutely love to fly. From the take off to the landing, I just love it. Also, I love sitting over the wing. I don't have a full reason why; I just like it for some reason. I like to watch all the different flaps and gears being adjusted on the wing as the pilot prepares the aircraft for takeoff. I also like to sit in the window seat and look at the sky, just over the tip of the wing. I love the feeling of being lifted off the ground as we take off. As the plane ascends into the air, it's as if the weight of the world drops off both the plane and me too. It's like I am suspended in the heavens with the angels. Of course, I'm still surrounded by ten tons of steel, but you get what I'm saying. The higher the pilot goes, the clearer the sky and the more pronounced is the sun.

One of the most beautiful things about the ascending is the ability to soar above any storms and clouds that are sometimes brooding over cities. What a beautiful sight! It's nothing like looking out of the window and seeing a sea of storms clouds, yet your face is warmed by the sun because of your position above it. Isn't that how the Father promises to do us in life? He causes us to soar above all that concerns us if we would but put our trust in Him. Looking down on the storm clouds reminds me of the line in the song, "Still." *"When the oceans rise and thunders roar / I will soar with you above the storm / Father, you are King over the flood / I will be still, know you are God."* And sometimes we need to do just that: SOAR, BE STILL and KNOW.

Oh, if only we would ascend with Him in the spirit. How do we do that? It's accomplished through prayer, praise, and worship. As we spend time in worship before Him, it takes us out of the soulish realm. It gets us off the ground. As we continue to worship, we begin to ascend until we are in the spiritual heavens with Him, far above the clouds and storms of life. And let me tell you, it's a different perspective from up there. The Son is always shining above the clouds. Always. When we spend time in worship and ascend with Him, we are reminded that He is King over the flood. There is no storm of life that cannot be overcome. Hallelujah!

If I could live in the sky, I probably would. Of course, I can't naturally do that, but there is nothing keeping me from living in the sky spiritually. It's our choice every day on whether we ascend with Him. We get to choose to soar with Him above our circumstances, issues, hurts, pains, and disappointments. It's a choice every day to step into that place of worship, prayer, and praise.

As I said, I love to fly, both naturally and spiritually. Whether you have ever taken a flight or not, you can choose to fly with the Father today. May you ascend high into the spiritual heavens as you spend time before Him!

Seated with Him

"And God raised us up with Christ and seated us with him in the heavenly realms in Christ Jesus, in order that in the coming ages he might show the incomparable riches of his grace, expressed in his kindness to us in Christ Jesus." ~Ephesians 2:6-7 NIV

I woke up very tender in my spirit. Whether I was thinking of the goodness of the Lord and His love for me, thinking and praying for friends, or worrying about the many financial issues that Albert and I were facing as a family, all of them seem to lead me to tears. All I wanted to do was lie at Jesus' feet and weep. Don't misunderstand. I was okay. I knew from walking with the Lord for over thirty years that the Lord was working on my heart, challenging me to a new place in Him. And although I was familiar with that place because I had been there quite a few times, my flesh always hates it. It's in those times of tenderness that I just want to stay home and be alone in His presence. There was no such luck; I could not dwell in the secret place that day.

In addition to going to meetings, appointments and running errands, I had to minister at my church that night. We were having a corporate prayer meeting and the leaders and elders were asked to pray prophetically for people at the service. I thought it may be best that I didn't minister to anyone, but not because I don't love ministry and people. It's because I take prayer and prophetic ministry so seriously that I did not want to be out of sync with the Spirit of the Lord and minister anything from my soulish realm. I pleaded my case with the Lord, but of course the Lord wasn't having it, so out of obedience I joined the ministers at the altar.

The whole time that I was praying and speaking to people I was feeling a little uneasy. Yet, I knew and could see the power of the Holy Spirit ministering to the hearts of the people who had come forth. As I was returned to my seat after the altar call, the Holy Spirit spoke to me. Our worship team was singing "Heaven On Earth," by David and Nicole Binion. One of the lines in the song says, "We're seated in heavenly places, just like heaven." That's when I heard the Holy Spirit speak clearly to me, "YOU ARE SEATED!" That shook my spirit!

I've sung that song so many times. In fact, I used to listen to it at least twice a day. I know the lyrics by heart. That's why I love it so much, but when the Holy Spirit spoke to me at church, I heard it so differently. I could hear and see the Lord himself, looking me in the eye and saying, "You are seated!" It was a rhema word for me.

The word *seated* implies a place of authority and power. The Lord was saying to me that, in Him, I walk in authority and power. He was reminding me that my experience, my wavering feelings, and emotions don't change or dictate my position in Him. The word says that the gifts and calling of God are without repentance. (Romans 11:29) His ability to move through me had nothing to do with my feelings and emotions. Praise God! I am seated in heavenly places with Him.

No matter how you're feeling today, know that it's only temporal. Remember that you are His and that you can stand on His promises. (2 Corinthians 1:20) Remember that you belong to the King of kings and the Lord of lords. You are a Chosen Generation, a Royal Priesthood, a Holy Nation, and a Peculiar People. Remember that you are seated (positioned) in heavenly places with Him!

Obedience is Key

"But Samuel replied, "What is more pleasing to the Lord: your burnt offerings and sacrifices or your obedience to his voice? Listen! Obedience is better than sacrifice, and submission is better than offering the fat of rams."
~I Samuel 15:22 NLT

Many times, the Father will speak to me in songs, usually to stir me and to get my attention to hear what He really wants to speak. He dropped "Lord, Sabaoth" by Robert Gay in my spirit one morning. It's an old, but powerful song.

Lord, Saboath
Lord of Host, Mighty in Battle
Lord, Saboath
Lord of the Armies of God

This was one of those songs that I would do spiritual battle within my personal prayer time. I would dance this song before the Lord and would literally weld my spiritual sword at the enemy. The Holy Spirit taught me years ago how to war, not only with my words of prayer, but also with my physical body. Little did I know that I would be dancing for the Lord later in life. I had a banner on my wall that had one of my favorite scriptures inscribed on it. One of my closest and dearest friends had it made for me many moons ago. It said, **"Blessed be the Lord my strength which teacheth my hands to war, and my fingers to fight." (Psalms 144:1)** I was destined to be a warrior!

I recall one time, out of obedience to the Holy Spirit, I was dancing around my room, boxing, and beating the air like Rocky Balboa swinging at the enemy. Man, I felt like a crazy fool in my flesh, but I could sense

the power of the Holy Spirit breaking forth in the spirit realm. ***"For the weapons of our warfare are not carnal, but mighty through God to the pulling down of strongholds." (II Corinthians 10:4)*** Now, mind you, this was before my praise dancing days. There was no such thing as a "praise dance" team, only the choir and praise and worship team existed, and I was a member of both. In that season, I was desperate for a breakthrough in my marriage, my children, and my ministry.
Intercession was my weapon of war. I obeyed the Holy Spirit's direction every day, not knowing that He was killing two birds with one stone. He was bringing breakthrough to all that I had prayed for, while preparing me for future things--such a time as this.

    Who would've thought that dancing around like a crazy woman in my bedroom thirty years ago was preparing me to be the dance director for four church campuses, six dance teams, and over 100 dancers, and still growing? Who would've thought that in twenty plus years' time I would have had the privilege of ministering to thousands of men and women, and continue to do so? Who would have thought that this abused and broken young girl would have the privilege of writing to you today? Only the Father God who is rich in mercy and grace knew. (Read Jeremiah 1:5)

    People of God, you have no idea what the Holy Spirit may be preparing you for, and really, you need not be concerned. You are only required to trust and obey. ***"...Eye hath not seen, nor ear heard, neither have entered into the heart of man, the things which God hath prepared for them that love him." (I Corinthians 2:9)***

    You may not be seeing the fruit right now but know that fruit is in your belly. In every seed, the word of God in you, there is a vine or tree that will bear fruit in its season. (Psalm 1:3) Your job is to be obedient when the Holy Spirit is giving you instructions, even if it seems a little crazy to your flesh. Know that you are sowing into your future.

    If He says to read your word every day, read it! If He says get up and pray at 4:00 am, pray! If He says dance before Him, then dance! Our obedience to the Lord is the key to our deliverance and victory over whatever we may be facing in this season: finances, jobs, children, ministry, neighbors, you name it. The Word of God is clear: If ye be willing AND obedient, ye shall eat (prosper, excel, accelerate) the good (the fruit, substance) of the land (naturally and spiritually). (Isaiah 1:19)

"...and your Father Who sees in secret will reward you openly. Also when you pray, you must not be like the hypocrites, for they love to pray standing in the synagogues and on the corners of the streets, that they may be seen by people. Truly I tell you, they have their reward in full already. But when you pray, go into your [most] private room, and, closing the door, pray to your Father, Who is in secret; and your Father, Who sees in secret, will reward you in the open." ~Matthew 6:4-6 AMPC

Private obedience will always bring public victory. Sometimes we want God to put us out front when often we are not ready. We are still struggling with obeying Him in secret, in the small things. In the Song of Solomon, it speaks of the little foxes that come to spoil the vine. Disobedience is a little fox. Examine your heart and see if you are allowing little foxes to spoil your vine, your love relationship with Jesus. It could be the key to your breakthrough.

What has God told you to do today? What has the Holy Spirit been prompting in your Spirit? Does it seem crazy and foolish? Maybe He asked you to extend your prayer time? Maybe He asked you to start a prayer time? Maybe He's told you to war in dance while you pray. Or maybe He's told you to sing love songs to Him, and you don't think you can sing. Maybe He's asked you to intercede on behalf of your leaders, both spiritual and natural. Or maybe He's asked you to give, even sacrificially to someone anonymously. Maybe He told you to purchase a gift for that person you can't stand. Or maybe He's told you to just lay prostrate before Him in silence.

I don't know what the Lord has required of you, or will require, but this I do know -- obedience is key!

Expectation & Hunger Fulfilled

"Blessed are they which do hunger and thirst after righteousness: for they shall be filled." ~Matthew 5:6 KJV

*"I'm walking on sunshine, oh-oh.
I'm walking on sunshine, oh-oh.
I'm walking on sunshine, oh-oh!
And don't it feel good?!"*

This song came to mind as I tried to think of words to describe what I was feeling after attending dance camp. The only difference was that I was singing SONshine instead of sunshine. I've attended the camp with our youth dance team, Wildfire, for many years. Each year, we came back exhausted from dancing with over ten hours of training all weekend. We also left refreshed and inspired in our spirit from being in the presence of the Lord. One particular year was no different as far as physically; I was exhausted. However, spiritually, the Father took me to another place.

Normally when I went to dance camp, in addition to all the administrative responsibilities, my focus was on Wildfire ministering under the anointing and power of God at the annual showcase. Much of my time and focus was on interceding in prayer, making sure costumes are in place, and handling administrative things so that Wildfire could be focused on being prepared vessels. Each year my heart's desire was that the Father would show Himself mighty through Wildfire and touch the hearts of all who come to see them. The Father never disappointed. He always took the two little fish and five loaves of bread of dance skills and fed the multitude.

I loved dance camp, but that year was a little different for me. Although I was still focused on Wildfire, their dance, and the necessary administrative responsibilities, my heart was in a different place. I went with an expectation. An expectation of what, you ask? I was not sure. I was just expecting something from the Father. I was looking for something more than the usual touch from Him during the services. The expectation, even hunger, in me was so strong that it was calling from deep within me. Even my prayer request at the early morning prayer meeting was that this expectation and hunger be fulfilled this weekend not only in me, but in all the dancers that attended with me. And again, the Father was faithful. I can't even begin to tell you all the things that took place; it's more than I have space or time here to share. Just know that He fulfilled that expectation. And it was exceedingly, abundantly, above all that I could have asked or thought.

Is there an expectation and hunger in your heart for God? Do you feel a stirring within you, drawing you toward Him? I want to encourage you to give attention to that hunger within. It's the Holy Spirit trying to stir something in you. Hunger for God is a good thing. The Bible says, **"Blessed are they which do hunger and thirst after righteousness: for they shall be filled." (Matthew 5:6)** It's a promise. Seek the Lord and cry out to Him. He will answer.

Maybe you don't have that expectation or hunger within you today. Maybe you're feeling just the opposite with a "whatever" or "I don't care" attitude. I want to encourage you to repent to the Lord for those attitudes. They are faith killers and will cause you to rebel against God. I want to encourage you to ask the Father to give you an expectation and a hunger for Him, His word, and the things that He desires. I'm a living testimony that He will answer. I was not always seeking after Him, but one day I got tired of where I was and wanted more of Him. I began to pray to the Father to give me a hunger for Him and for His word, and He did. Every day it increases in intensity. Hallelujah!

I pray that the Father increases your expectation and hunger today and that you will see the fulfilling of those expectations in the days ahead. I want you to be able to sing with me: *"I'm walking on SONshine, oh-oh. I'm walking on SONshine, oh-oh. I'm walking on SONshine, oh-oh. And don't it feel good?!"*

It Gets Smaller

"Therefore if any man be in Christ, he is a new creature: old things are passed away; behold, all things are become new." ~II Corinthians 5:17 KJV

One of my favorite television shows is *Burn Notice*, a series that used to come on the USA network. The show was about a former CIA operative, Michael Westin, who had been given a "burn notice." That simply meant that he was fired and no longer allowed to work for the CIA. The weekly series was about him trying to find out who fired him and why and his attempt to get back into the CIA. There's so much more to the show, but that's the gist of it.

My husband and I were watching it together one evening. The main character, Michael, had messed up with his two partners: Fiona, his girlfriend and Sam, his best friend. An old acquaintance of Michael's suddenly showed up, wreaking havoc and causing trouble, pushing him to compromise some of his standards as a spy. His two partners could see that it was a cantankerous relationship for him, even warning him, but Michael wasn't hearing it. The long and short of it is that they parted ways, leaving Michael to handle the acquaintance by himself. When things fell apart, which they did very quickly, Michael needed his friends to help fix things. This meant that he had to apologize.

Michael made an apology to Sam and Fiona together, but I just loved what he specifically said to Fiona. While explaining his reasons for not heeding her warning about the acquaintance, he said, "There's a part of me that's like him [referring to the old acquaintance], but it's just a part, and it gets smaller the longer I'm with you." What a line! Michael was basically saying that although he could relate to some of the ways of this old acquaintance, that the gap between what was and what is widened the more time he spent with Fiona. Think about that. What are your relationships bringing out of you? Are they bringing out the best or the worst?

I thought about how my love for my husband, my children, and my grandson makes me desire to be a better wife, mother, and grandmother. I thought about how my love for dance, my dancers, and my students compel and press me to not be lazy, to dance hard, choreograph well, and purpose to always be at my best. I thought about the wonderful women, spiritual daughters, and dear friends that the Father has graced me to know and how my love for them presses me to live godly before them, purposing to display the love of Christ in all that I do. And I thought about my love for my Lord and Savior Jesus Christ and that the more time that I spend with Him, the deeper my love for Him grows, and the wider the gap becomes between the old me and new me.

I can relate to the Michael character. So often I can see a side of me that is very real, but that is not like Christ at all. Sometimes that part of me, that fleshly nature, rises and even pushes me to compromise and do things that are not pleasing to the Lord. I know that side of me exists and that I need the grace and mercy of the Holy Spirit every day to help me to not compromise. This is the plight of the saints, our daily war: ***"For the flesh lusteth against the Spirit, and the Spirit against the flesh: and these are contrary the one to the other." (Galatians 5:17)***

However, the Father did not leave us defenseless. He has given us the Holy Spirit to walk with us and lead us into all truth. (John 16:13) I am thankful to the Lord that a part of the old me dies every day as I spend time with my Father, as I spend time in His word, and as I allow the Holy Spirit to minister to my heart. That side of me that wants to compromise becomes less and less. When I am in His presence, His love, that is so gentle and kind, compels me to let go of the old and embrace the new creature that I am in Christ Jesus.

Listen, nobody knows you better than yourself (accept Jesus, of course). There are thoughts and feelings inside of your hearts that no one ever sees or hears. Thank God! Yet, the Father knows. And if you're like me, you don't want those thoughts and ways to define who you are. I want to encourage you to take time to get in His presence and allow the Father to love on you every day. I promise that you and everyone around you will see and know the difference in your daily walk. There will be less of you and more of Him.

I pray that you will know His love and presence today. I pray that His Love will draw you closer to Him and further from thoughts and ways of your flesh. I pray that His love for you will give you a deep desire to know Him and want to please Him. I pray that your relationships are bringing out the best in you and drawing you toward Christ. I pray that you will not compromise today, but that you will be compelled to love Him in all that you do.

He Goes Before You

"The Lord himself goes before you and will be with you; he will never leave you nor forsake you. Do not be afraid; do not be discouraged." ~Deuteronomy 31:8 NIV

I was lying in the bed awake early one morning, meditating on the word and talking to the Lord. I was going over a dream that I had the night before. This is something I do every morning while things are fresh in my mind. I listened for the Holy Spirit to reveal any issues of my heart, which are often revealed through my dreams. I was also praising and thanking the heavenly Father for His faithfulness to Albert and me concerning our home.

    A few weeks back we had received a letter from our mortgage company, stating that we were delinquent in our payments and were on the verge of going into foreclosure, possibly losing our home. There had been an internal miscommunication within the company, but of course, when that happens, the burden of proof lies upon the customer. For two weeks, the mortgage company had us jumping through hoops, some that we had already jumped through months prior. It was a very stressful process, not because of the things they required of us, but because of the power they seemed to hold over our lives. I did not like the fact that although we did all that was necessary to prove our "innocence," it was, seemingly, still going to be up to them whether we were exonerated. It was not a cool situation at all.

    I don't want to bore you with all the details, but in the end, My Father was once again faithful. We received a letter apologizing for the late fees that had been accessed to our mortgage. The letter stated that they reviewed our track record and could see that we had been faithful customers. Not only did the letter indicate that we were no longer considered delinquent, but they made sure to remove all late fees and charges. Hallelujah!

So, there I was, lying in the dark, thinking on all of that and praising the Lord. I was thanking Him for once again causing us to triumph over yet another battle. Although I was happy and rejoicing over that victory, my heart kind of half rejoiced for a second as my mind began to drift to all the other battles that still needed to be fought. It was as if I was rejoicing in my spirit, but my head slightly turned and caught a glance of a stack of battles that were still pending.

But oh, how I just love Jesus! Right when I felt my heart sinking, the Holy Spirit began to speak. He said to me, "He goes before you!" It was almost as if He were saying, "What are you fretting over? He's got this and He's got you!" I began to really ponder and meditate on those words as they continued to ring repeatedly and loudly in my spirit. "He goes before me! He's got this! And He's got ME!"

I began to take heart and rejoice once again. I love the Lord with all my heart, and I love the fact that He always sends words to encourage and comfort my soul and spirit. I was reminded through that simple phrase that it is He is faithful. (Hebrews 10:23) I was reminded that it is He who goes before us to fight our battles. (II Chronicles 32:8) It is He who brings vindication and justification to those who are in Christ Jesus. (Romans 4:25 & I Corinthians 1:30) It is He who holds the heart of earthly kings in His hand and turns it, as water, whithersoever He wills. (Proverbs 21:1) It is He whose favor and grace rest upon us and causes us to have favor with God and Man. And I was reminded that it is He who causes us to triumph in all things. (II Corinthians 2:14) I need not fear what man can do to me (Psalm 118:6), because the battle is not mine, but it's the Lord.

"This day will the Lord deliver thee into mine hand; and I will smite thee, and take thine head from thee; and I will give the carcases of the host of the Philistines this day unto the fowls of the air, and to the wild beasts of the earth; that all the earth may know that there is a God in Israel. And all this assembly shall know that the Lord saveth not with sword and spear: for the battle is the Lord's, and he will give you into our hands." ~I Samuel 17:46-47 KJV

People of God, take courage! Be bold as King David was when he went up against the uncircumcised Philistines. I loved when he said to his enemy, "This day will the Lord deliver you into my hands." I don't know what battle you may be facing, but I pray that the spirit of King David, the worship warrior, will be upon you today and that you will speak to your enemy knowing that the Lord has given him into your hands. Remember, the Word says that our enemy is as a roaring lion (I Peter 5:8), but our God, who is the Lord of host and the Lord of many armies, is Jesus. He is our Lion of Judah. Hallelujah!

Find rest, peace, and victory in Him today!

Be On Guard

"Be alert and of sober mind. Your enemy the devil prowls around like a roaring lion looking for someone to devour." ~I Peter 5:8 NIV

There's nothing like being in the presence of the Lord. It is so refreshing to your soul and spirit. In His presence, I find solace, peace, joy, forgiveness and restoration and there is a love so pure that it is tangible, surrounding and embracing me, bringing comfort and security to all that concerns me. It is in His presence that I go back to the cross at Calvary and realize His great love for me. It is in His presence that my mountains become pebbles of sand as I am reminded of His great majesty and awesomeness. *There is none like you, O Lord.*

"Who is like unto thee, O LORD, among the gods? Who is like thee, glorious in holiness, fearful in praises, doing wonders?" ~Exodus 15:11 KJV

Whenever I set out to do something for the kingdom, it is expected that the spiritual warfare in my life will increase tremendously. The more I share, the more I am challenged to walk by the spirit of the Lord. The more I am challenged, the more I realize that this is not a game. Our enemy is real, but our God is greater!

I remember when I first started my blog years ago and shortly after the launch, I was blindsided by the enemy. It was kind of my fault. The Word says in James 1:19, "…let every man be swift to hear, slow to speak, slow to wrath." It's a warning to be careful not to react in our flesh or our old, sinful nature. Well, I missed the mark on that day.

I had a situation that came up. It was one that had been ongoing for quite some time and basically, I was sick of it. I wanted it to go away and was tired of "letting the powers that be" deal with it, especially since it seemed that they were not "handling" it too well. I decided that I was going to take matters into my own hands and deal with the situation myself, hopefully putting an end to it once and for all. That was my first mistake.

I tried to deal with the situation in what I thought was a diplomatic way. However, because my intent to mend was not spirit-led, it ended up making matters worse. When I was confronted with the mess that I had made by "handling" the issue, my reaction was not too godly to say the least. I became defensive to the point of making myself out to be the victim of it all. Rather than humbling myself and apologizing, I allowed the enemy to feed me one thought: "They just don't appreciate you." And you know what? I swallowed the bait. Hook, line and sinker! That was mistake number two!

Instead of casting the thought down, as the Word of God says, I allowed that thought from the enemy to permeate my soul and spirit by dwelling on it. Mistake number three. The more I thought about being "underappreciated," the more thoughts came that were reinforcing the *so-called* fact. Of course, my perception was all thwarted because of my anger and lack of humility. Within twenty minutes, that one thought had snowballed into a mountain of defeat. When all was said and done, not only was I hurt and angry, but I thought my life was a huge mess. How did I get there from one thought? I will tell you how--not obeying the Word.

There is a real enemy who is out to KILL, STEAL, and DESTROY! (John 10:10) Don't be fooled. The devil is a worthy foe. If it were not for the grace and mercy of the Father and the wisdom of the Holy Spirit, we would all be defeated. It is vitally important that we obey God's word. **"For the wages of sin is death; but the gift of God is eternal life through Jesus Christ our Lord." (Romans 6:23)**

To make a long story short, I finished the night very quietly. I've walked with the Lord long enough to know that I had gone down a wrong road and that the best way to keep from totally crashing was to be silent before Him. *SELAH.*

I turned in early and awoke the next morning anxious to get into His presence. As I entered prayer and worship, my heart cried out to my Father for comfort. I laid my plight before Him, asking Him all the "why me" questions. The Father, who is so rich in mercy, responded in gentleness and grace. He brought a song to my remembrance called, "Make Me Invisible." I could hear the lyrics in my head as the Holy Spirit took me through the events of the previous day. The Holy Spirit showed me just how the enemy got me. He showed me the moment when I let my guard down. He showed me how, in my moment of weakness, the enemy was able to get me focused inward, instead of upward. This shift in focus opened an immediate door for the enemy to go for the juggler.

You see, the enemy is not out just to injure you; his goal is to take you totally out. He wants to kill your marriage, your children, and your influence. He will wait for the most opportune time to pounce on you. That's why it is so important that we daily put on the armor of God (Ephesians 6:13-18), that we guard our hearts with all diligence (Proverbs 4:23), and that we walk in the spirit so that we don't fulfill the lust (desires) of the flesh (Galatians 5:16). This is a matter of LIFE and DEATH!

Praise God for His faithfulness to us despite ourselves. I am thankful that we can find grace, mercy, and forgiveness in His presence. I am thankful that He not only forgives, but that He restores. And I am thankful that it is not about me, but all about Him. I am re-focused today, are you?

"But thanks be to God, which giveth us the victory through our Lord Jesus Christ." ~I Corinthians 15:17 KJV

May you find grace, mercy, and wisdom as you dwell in His presence today!

Let His Glory Arise!

"Arise, shine; for thy light is come, and the glory of the Lord is risen upon thee." ~Isaiah 60:1 KJV

The Holy Spirit dropped a song in my spirit one evening that I just couldn't stop singing. The song is called "Let It Rise" by William Murphy III.

> *Let the glory of the Lord rise among us*
> *Let the glory of the Lord rise among us*
> *Let the praises of our King rise among us*
> *Let it rise*
> *Oh, let it rise*
>
> *Let the songs of the Lord rise among us*
> *Let the songs of the Lord rise among us*
> *Let the joy of our King rise among us*
> *Let it rise*
> *Oh, let it rise*

I hadn't heard that song in quite some time, so when I heard it bellowing up from my belly, I knew it was the Lord speaking to me. The Word of God says that, out of your belly shall flow rivers of living water. (John 7:38) Get that! The Lord will bring a word of deliverance and freedom from your own belly. *SELAH.*

I began to sing the chorus to this song repeatedly as I rode along in the car. As I sang, I could feel the presence of the Lord rising in me and around me. The Holy Spirit began to speak to me, bringing to my remembrance the scripture that I'm sure this song is based on.

"Arise, shine; for thy light is come, and the glory of the Lord is risen upon thee. For, behold, the darkness shall cover the earth, and gross darkness the people: but the LORD shall arise upon thee, and his glory shall be seen upon thee." ~Isaiah 60:1-2 KJV

In this passage of scripture, the children of Israel had once again been in captivity. The Father God sent word through the prophet Isaiah that He was once again delivering them from their captivity and bringing restoration. Not only was the Lord God, in His infinite mercy and grace, restoring them once again, but He was also allowing His glory to shine and rest upon them. The Greek word for glory in this passage is *chabod* (pronounced kah-vohd). *Chabod* means weightiness, heavy, substance; it also means glory, splendor, honor, power, wealth, authority, magnificence, fame, dignity, riches, and excellency. Think about that for a minute. What a powerful act of the Father God to allow His glory (His substance, authority, wealth, fame, power, etc....) to cover His people. We serve an awesome God!

The prophet Isaiah told the children of Israel that His glory would cover them, even when darkness was all around. That sounds like the times we're living in. In other words, when others can't see and are spiritually blind, lost, hopeless, and can't seem to find their way, His people would not be in darkness. (I Thessalonians 4:13) His glory would be over them during it all. Praise be to God!

I know the Lord was speaking to me and encouraging my heart. Life had been pressing pretty hard for a few years, few months, and few days. The shadow of the enemy had been large and luminous. And although I knew deep in my spirit that the Lord had me and all that concerned me, at times fear would try to overwhelm me. That morning was no different. I found myself concerned with the "how" and "when" of my situation. *How are you going to do it Lord and when, when, when?*

As I meditated on the song and the Word of God, my spirit man began to rejoice! The Lord was reassuring me that He was bringing restoration to me, my situation, my dreams, my hopes. His glory was shining upon me. Even amid the darkness, He was causing His glory to be upon me. The Spirit of the Lord was speaking loud and clear. It's a new season. It's a new day. A fresh anointing has come my way. Hallelujah!

Embrace this word for yourself because God is no respecter of persons. (Romans 2:11) I don't know what you're facing in your life and circumstances right now, but I want to encourage your heart today. Meditate on this word and take it as your own. Sing this song out loud. Declare it for yourself. Let the glory of the Lord rise among you, among your situation, among your finances, your marriage, and your health. Let the glory of the Lord arise! Hallelujah!

I Feel Like Running

"But they that wait upon the Lord shall renew their strength; they shall mount up with wings as eagles; they shall run, and not be weary; and they shall walk, and not faint." ~Isaiah 40:31 KJV

I woke up one Tuesday morning with a full schedule ahead of me. I started the day handling necessary business for our Resurrection Sunday dance. Then I got my hair done, cleaned, cooked, washed, and worked on finishing my homework for school, all in addition to scheduling a job interview and writing. Although I was praising God for the warm temperatures and sunshine, the cares of the day seem to be closing in on me. I was getting things done, but there was a part of me that just wanted to be going somewhere or doing something else. That thought seemed to intensify as the day went on.

One of my errands was to take care of some paperwork at my church, which I did. As I was driving through the forest preserve en route back to my home, the thought of wanting to go and be elsewhere arose again. As I looked out at the open fields that surrounded me, I had this unexplainable urge to run. I could literally hear myself saying, "I feel like running." I just wanted to run. I couldn't shake the feeling. I wanted to pull the car over, get out, and run through one of the fields that surrounded me as fast and far as I could go. Of course, I didn't but I imagined myself running as hard as I could, hearing my heart beating rapidly in my chest, feeling the wind blowing on my perspiring face, and smiling as I enjoyed the freedom.

The desire to run took me back to my middle and high school days as a track runner. I was a sprinter in middle school and ran the 100-meter and 400-meter dashes, relay, and did shot-put in high school. I absolutely loved track and everything about it, from our two-hour practices every day to our weight training and especially the track meets. It's something about finishing a run that was refreshing to the spirit. It didn't matter that I was out of breath and my chest hurt from the mere intensity of the run. It didn't matter that my sides and legs would cramp at times, having to wait an hour until the pain subsided. It didn't matter that I would be exhausted after a full-day track meet. It was all about the run. Yet, even with my love for my running days, I still couldn't understand why I was feeling a sudden urge to run so intensely. Then the Holy Spirit began to speak to my heart (You should know by now that there's always a lesson!)

I believe the desire to run was two-fold. The first was my desire to escape the cares of this world that can easily overtake us at times. That has always been one of the busiest times of year for me and it's not unusual for me to do the many things that are required during that season. However, that year, I felt very different when doing my "usual." It was almost as if the grace to get it done was being lifted. It was if I could sense that what defined me in years past no longer seemed to be fitting me. I was growing "out my britches," if you will. The urgency to run was the Holy Spirit prompting a desire in me to move without fear and hesitation into the things that He had set before me.

The Holy Spirit reminded of one of the words that the Lord had given me for the year: acceleration. I believe that there is a great acceleration in the spirit that the Father is positioning and repositioning many in the body of Christ. It's as if a strong wind is blowing as it did when the Father God parted the Red Sea: ***"...and the LORD caused the sea to go back by a strong east wind all that night, and made the sea dry land, and the waters were divided." (Exodus 14:21b***) Open doors and opportunities are being released to the body of Christ in this hour.

Don't get me wrong. I didn't drop everything that I was doing and start running to unknown places and people without the explicit direction and confirmation of the Holy Spirit and you shouldn't do that either. I believe that the urge to run was a way the Father was preparing me for what's to come, for that which was before me. This leads to my second reason for the urgency to run.

I also believe that the Father was and is calling many to go forth in their gift and callings by the leading of the Holy Spirit. It's time to run! The Holy Spirit brought back to my remembrance a dream that one of my spiritual daughters had a few years ago. I won't attempt to go into the details of the dream here, but I want to share the portion that shot through my mind concerning the running. In the dream, she and I were standing at the edge of an open field. Suddenly, she looked at me and I at her. There were some words spoken that indicated that I needed to run and so I did, immediately. I took off running in the field as fast as I could go. Then she took off right after me. Now, this is probably insignificant to most, but for me it was speaking volumes. The Lord was, again, reminding me that time to run was upon me. The message was simple: be prepared.

I know that the Father had me incubated for a season. He was personally working on me by the Holy Spirit: breaking, pruning, restructuring, adjusting, and rebuilding. During that time, my husband and I began journeying into a season of restoration and renewal. The desire to run was a part of that debut and the acceleration took place in the spirit.

The Father is stirring the hearts of those who are His, yours and mine. He is stirring His people, as a mother eagle does her eaglets. She makes their nest uncomfortable in hopes of them embracing their God-ordained destiny to fly. The Father is preparing His people, as the mother eagle prepares the eaglet, to be dropped from the nest located at the peak of the mountaintop. The Father, just as the mother eagle, fully expects us to spread our wings and fly and be the eagles we were destined to be, soaring above all.

I don't know about you, but I feel the stirring, acceleration, and urgency all around. What is the spirit of the Lord stirring in you? What is He stirring you to? Do you sense the urgency in the spirit? The Father is calling His people in this hour. I believe that it is a season that the Father is raising up laborers for souls in the body of Christ. The scripture says, **"The harvest truly is plenteous, but the labourers are few." (Matthew 9:37)** I pray that you're seeking His heart today and that you will allow Him to accelerate you into the things of the kingdom.

Epilogue

When I look back over all the things that have happened in my life – the good, the bad, and the ugly – even in hindsight it's clear to see that God loves the perfectly imperfect. He was, and is, aware of all our flaws, our vices, our inhibitions, our fears, our thoughts (good and bad), our prejudices and our pride, *and still, He comes to us* (as the song writer said). It makes me wonder, what does He see that I don't see. Yet, every experience has proven that it's much more than I could ask or think. Truly, He has worked ALL things for my GOOD. Looking back, it is clear to see God's hand of love, grace, and mercy in my life. It is clear to see the work of the Holy Spirit meticulously scattered throughout my every day. It is clear to see that all things, although at times painful, challenging, and even humbling, have made me into the woman I am today. The word of God is true, *He who begun a good work in you **will be faithful** to complete it* (Philippians 1:6).

Yes, I am, we are, perfectly imperfect, and yet, there is a God that *still* loves me. God's love is simply AMAZING. HIS love is unconditional. HIS love is transforming. HIS love is empowering. HIS love pursues the unlovable. HIS love covers a multitude of sin. And most importantly, HIS love saves to the utmost. These pages reflect *that* love.

Maybe you're looking at your life right now and thinking, "*I don't have much to offer*" or "*What can God do with this mess?*" Let me tell you– more than you think. He truly can transform all things messy into something beautiful. I am living proof of that. I encourage you to continue to trust that He's in the midst of all things and that He's working all things for your good.

Maybe you don't know God. Maybe the probability of the Lord being concerned and involved in your everyday seems a bit far-fetched. Before you dismiss it all as fiction, I encourage you to get to know this God I'm speaking of. He desires to have a personal relationship with you and He's only waiting for your invitation.

The Bible says, *"**If you confess with your mouth the Lord Jesus and believe in your heart that God has raised Him from the dead, you will be saved.**" **(Romans 10:8-9)*** It's that simple. If you believe that, repeat this simple prayer: *Dear Lord Jesus, I know that I am a sinner, and I ask for Your forgiveness. I believe You died for my sins and rose from the dead. I turn from my sins and invite You to come into my heart and life. I want to trust and follow You as my Lord and Savior.***

Congratulations! You are now a born-again believer!

**For more information on this newfound life in Jesus and find a local Bible teaching church go here:
https://www.newlifenetwork.org/resources/new-believers/

Acknowledgements

Thank you to my patient and forbearing husband of 33 years, Albert P. Caldwell, who has both loved me through and endured this journey with me. I am the fly-in-the-wind tether ball and you are the grounded and steady anchor – yep, *Reese's* peanut butter cups forever. You are not, and never will be, taken for granted. Love you!

Thank you to my daughters, Katheryn, Alisha, Christina and Eudora, who have been my biggest fans and cheerleaders. Your words of encouragement and praise, your prayers, and the love you show me, despite me, give me fuel to live the life I live to its fullest that He might be glorified. I love you each and all, with depths that words fail to describe.

To my sons, Jonathan and Christopher, who I love unconditionally, know that I see the real you and it makes me smile. My heart's prayer is that you will know Him as I know Him and that you know that you are loved eternally. Proud *Momma Bear,* I am.

A special thank you to my brother and friend, Pastor-Apostle-Prophet Samuel Hamstra, who believed in the God in me when no one else would and took a chance on me when no one else would. Thank you for always allowing me to be me. Your gift of friendship and leadership is invaluable. It is a true honor and joy to be serving the body of Christ and our Lord together. Love you!

Meet the Author

Dorothy Caldwell is the Chaplain for the WNBA Chicago Sky and has been privileged to minister to WNBA players throughout the league and the administrative staff for the past 11 years. She is a licensed and ordained minister and has been serving the body of Christ through word and dance for over 30 years. She is a mentor, spiritual mother & sister, counselor, and friend to many and counts it an honor to serve others. **Dorothy** is the founder of *D. Caldwell Ministries*, a ministry established and designed to educate, empower, and encourage men and women toward their God-ordained life purposes through sound biblical teaching, strong Godly mentorship, consistent discipleship, and through the ministry of dance and other forms of the performing arts. **Dorothy** is a wife, a mother of 6, and grandmother of 8. She and her husband, Albert, of 33 years are the founders and owners of *Wellspring Creative Services*, where they have been privileged to teach music, dance, and fitness to students of all ages for the past 15 years. Together, they serve over 400 students throughout the Chicagoland area every week. **Dorothy** has ministered in word and dance throughout the United States, the Philippines, and abroad. She purposes to bring glory and honor to God in **all** that she does (Matthew 5:16), and no matter where she goes, or who she meets, NOTHING compares, nor can take the place of, her family or her relationship with her **audience of One, Jesus Christ!**

www.ingramcontent.com/pod-product-compliance
Lightning Source LLC
Chambersburg PA
CBHW070948080526
44587CB00015B/2233